Blue-Collar Riches

How to transform minimum wage into maximum wealth

Montgomery Sterling McGale

Book Layout © 2018 BookDesignTemplates.com

Blue-Collar Riches/Montgomery Sterling McGale. -- 1st ed.
ISBN 978-1507701287
ISBN 1507701284

To the few that will

Contents

Plan

At first glance these ten rules will seem quite simple, yet they are the distillation from decades of experience and observation. Aimed specifically at young, blue-collar workers that earn minimal wages, these rules are a guide to build wealth and establish lasting habits that will ensure you always deal from a strength.

Each rule will be explained and later chapters will contain many examples of real-world successes and failures. The ten rules are:

1. Set and achieve R.A.W. goals.

2. Live as cheap as possible for two years.

3. Save as much money as possible in two years.

4. Develop a marketable skill and expertise.

5. Start making deals.

6. Deal from a position of strength.

7. Never use Deal Bag money for living.

8. Align yourself with like-minded people.

9. Take advantage of macroeconomics.

10. Don't quit your day job till you are ready.

Curious about the rules? Still interested in transforming your minimum wage into maximum wealth? Willing to put forth effort toward improving your life? Serious about creating a solid financial empire? Yes? Please continue.

Chapter Two

Rules

Rule number one: Set and achieve RAW goals.

Most people float through life, never reaching their potential, merely wishing for change, whereas the ability to establish goals and achieve them is one of the best skills to develop; it will serve you for the rest of your life. There are numerous books and guides dealing with motivation and goals. I was fortunate as a young man to learn a simple system that anyone can put into practice. It is the R. A. W. system.

1. Realistic

2. Attainable

3. Worthwhile

Three criteria that every goal you set should conform to, that is, if you are serious about accomplishing your objective. Ask yourself if the goal you are contemplating is Realistic? Attainable? Worthwhile? As you scrutinize the guidelines in Blue-Collar Riches, inevitably you'll ask yourself if living frugally for two years, saving money, learning an expertise and making deals is realistic. Can it be done? Is it worth the effort?

To make the big picture easier to understand and/or accomplish, let's break it into components. Is it reasonable (realistic) that a twenty-something person can live frugally and save money? Has anyone ever done this? Of course; thousands of people throughout history (and all around the world) have realized the value in living a thrifty lifestyle in order to save money for a large goal. You may even know someone who sacrificed for six months to save money to go on a backpacking trip for three months to Thailand. People do it all the time. Laying low for two years to save twenty-five thousand dollars is very realistic.

Has any blue-collar worker ever attained such a goal when earning minimum wage? The answer is yes.

Many people have accomplished that, and more. You are not breaking new ground or embarking on a course of action that is impossible.

Can a passion-based level of skill be developed while saving money? A skill that can be put to use in profitable dealmaking? Yes and yes. Teaching yourself a skill is quite attainable. You won't be the first or last person to knuckle down and train themselves in a passionate pursuit that can be turned into profit.

Is the goal of financial strength and long-term fiscal security for you and your family worthwhile? Of course it is.

Some say that money doesn't buy happiness; that may be true, by the same reasoning, lack of money buys even less happiness. Being in control of your monetary situation is a worthwhile goal; living as a debt-slave is to exist as a victim. You don't want that.

The objectives of sacrifice, saving, learning and making deals to build lasting financial strength fulfill all the criteria of R. A. W. goals.

Next step is to reduce a large goal into smaller pieces that are easier to accomplish. 'Save twenty-five thousand dollars in two years' can seem like a daunting task. Saving a thousand dollars each month is much easier to wrap your head around. Five hundred dollars from each biweekly paycheque earmarked for a saving's account will start to add up quickly. That is one of the techniques in managing goals: reducing large objectives into smaller pieces. Yearly, monthly, weekly, and even daily targets of how much money should flow into savings, food, fuel, and other costs of living can be calculated when a large goal is divided into manageable bits.

Another habit to establish that will help accomplish any goal: write it down. Goals need to be committed to paper, physically written in a dedicated notebook, not on a computer screen or in a smart phone. This is crucial. A goal not written is merely a wish. Your goals need to be in a special notebook or agenda, and it needs to be placed in a visible location where it can be seen often. The book with your goals must be a constant reminder and be visible to people that are involved with your life. Correct, your goals need to be made public, especially to those people you work (and associate) with. Why? Simple; it is an extra level of motivation.

True motivation comes from within, but it is often very helpful to have people in your life that will serve as reminders to accomplish what you set out to do. Not all will be supportive; some will tease, cajole, ridicule, tell you how crazy you are, or even laugh and scoff. Their peer pressure and comments may start as snide remarks when they are initially informed of your intentions. Some won't understand why you won't be purchasing an expensive Frappa-mochaccino every morning, but, I can assure you, remarks from coworkers and friends will turn to admiration as you stick to your goal and (Deal Bag) savings accumulate.

Another way to remind yourself to stay on track; keep your major-savings-goal in your wallet. On a slip of paper write the specific objective, it might say, "Twenty-four thousand dollars saved in twenty-four months." Each time you open your wallet, there it is, your Realistic, Attainable, Worthwhile goal. Pretty soon you won't need a reminder to stay on track with your disciplined budget. New habits will be formed. You will be capable of eliminating wasteful spending and honing the ability to cut corners. Preparing your own meals, packing your lunch, buying quality used clothing at thrift-stores, car-pooling or cycling — the list is practically endless where money can be saved.

Practice the process of RAW goals, even on a small scale.

In your book of goals jot down Saturday morning's objective for your workout at the gym (make sure it is RAW) and on the way out the door tell a roommate exactly what you are going to do. He or she will ask you later if you accomplished your workout goal. Simple way of providing an extra level of motivation. Reward yourself with a pat on the back and write down in your goal-book you accomplished the gym's objective. If you didn't, step back and figure out why. Was your workout target unrealistic in its numbers? Did you set an unattainable level for yourself? When your roommate asked about your workout did you lie to him?

Setting and achieving goals will become second nature as you practice the process. This will be one of the best habits you can develop and will serve you in a positive way for the rest of your life. RAW goals will ensure your wishes of self improvement and financial security will become reality.

Setting and achieving RAW goals is rule number one for a reason... every objective that helps build your character and establish a position of wealth will stem from an ability to accomplish goals. This is the key that will open the door to success, wealth and a great amount of happiness as you incorporate the principles of RAW goals into as many areas of your life as possible.

Rule Number Two: Live as cheap as possible for a minimum of two years.

Why two years? Twenty-four months will allow you to fully commit to a course of self-help; giving you plenty of time to establish new and profitable habits.

Most young peoples' largest monthly expense is rent. If that were eliminated or minimized, then money could be saved and put to work.

How cheaply can you live? I have rented living space that cost thirty-five dollars a month. At the same time most of my friends were paying eight hundred dollars (plus utilities) for an apartment. Rule number two is about living frugally for at least two years.

Thirty-five dollars a month rented me an old, single-car garage in the heart of a big city in British Columbia, Canada. Living in a rundown garage was quite comfortable and the landlord of the rooming house that the garage sat behind was happy I made my home there as he could count on me to help him with small repairs or an extra pair of hands to lighten his load when he (sometimes) needed assistance. He didn't mind that I tapped into the television cable or that my composting toilet's contributions enriched the little garden I grew in his backyard. As an absentee landlord he knew I was a phone call away and could be counted on to protect his interests.

Meanwhile, most of my friends spent the majority of their income on rent. How much? Simple math; with utilities, about a thousand dollars a month. In two years that is twenty-four grand. What could you do with that sum of money?

At the same time my thirty-five dollars per month was increased slightly by a two year membership at a nearby gym that cost five hundred dollars; a convenient place to shower. My shower cost less than twenty-one dollars a month. In comparison; my two year rental expense was less than fifteen hundred bucks. A far cry from the great sums of money most of my friends were paying to have a roof over their heads.

How much money did most of my friends save? Usually very little. Those that started families tended to take a very long time to save for a down payment to purchase their first property. Some had the luxury of in-laws' or parents' money to assist in a home-purchase when the first grandchild came along. Without such support, your goal should be to do everything within your ability to minimize your monthly living expenses and maximize your savings. Over a two-year period the amount can be impressive. (More on the topic in following chapters).

Use your imagination and creativity to find a solution that works for you. A couple more examples of living cheaply. The peak of a two-car garage (four-foot high attic space) was my sleeping quarters for three years. I called it the Squirrel's Nest. More than enough space to sleep. Even had television. The two car garage underneath the Squirrel's Nest cost me two hundred and twenty-five dollars a month. Income generated from my speciality metal-working business in the garage (more on that later) easily paid for the monthly rent in less than a day's effort. Friends called me crazy; let your buddies do the same while you create a sacrifice-living-situation that costs next to nothing.

Have rented a room in shared quarters with mates where a month cost two hundred dollars (plus utilities). Not bad; even managed a thirty-six-unit apartment building where I paid no rent but had to devote a few hours each day to routine maintenance and repairs. Majority of each day was dedicated to making money with cool cars (details in later chapters).

There are many ways to cut living expenses. Takes a little imagination and willingness to live 'abnormally'. Trade labour for a roof over your head. Many older people are living in large houses they can't afford to maintain, yet they are too stubborn or sentimental to sell and downsize. Offer to live in the basement or spare room in exchange for a certain number of work-hours per week: mowing the lawn, trimming hedges, gardening, shovelling snow, driving them for groceries. Set ground rules upfront; make sure everyone is happy with the arrangement.

Many businesses would like to have a person on the premises at night as security. Even if you occupy a cot in a corner, the boss will have peace of mind knowing there is a body on the property who can call proper authorities should something go bump in the night.

Live in a vehicle. A camper or a van, parked in a friend's backyard or even where you work. Just the presence of a vehicle that is occupied and sitting at your workplace is enough to send any troublemakers down the road. Your morning commute will be the envy of workmates.

Use your imagination, figure out how you can live as cheaply as possible. Your goal should be a minimum of two years. Which leads us to the purpose of the exercise...

Rule number three: Save as much money as possible.

Set a RAW goal and strive to achieve it. Even if your humble blue-collar job pays you one or two thousand dollars a month; if you're not paying the majority of that on rent each month, savings will add up very quick. Discipline and setting goals (see rule number one) are the key to success. Be careful; living like a cheap bugger can become addictive. Every time I have paid a normal rent (usually while living with a girlfriend or wife), it has always been short-lived and expensive.

This is a good time to speak of partners and saving money. I'm referring to a girlfriend, boyfriend, husband or wife. There seems to be little middle ground;

if you're with a partner, it is either a blessing or a curse (as far as saving money is concerned). Money; discussions on how it is to be earned and spent, can lead to heated debate. If you are presently with a partner and he or she is fully committed to the idea of sacrificing with you to save money, then you are very blessed, cherish that person.

What usually happens is the opposite. Direct experience has taught me that most women are not thrilled with the prospect of making a temporary home in a Squirrel's Nest. Even if the two years of frugal living could lead to a secure and comfortable future, most women won't do it.

Should you find yourself coupled with an individual that sees merit in your sacrifice-to-save-objective, you can do great things with your combined incomes. Economies of scale can be utilized: one vehicle instead of two. Food and its preparation time and cost are eased when approached as a team. Savings in time can be achieved when tasks are evenly divided. A cooperative approach to the goal of saving the maximum amount of money in twenty-four months will make the pair of you more united. Call the two years a refiner's fire, as you iron out details of your character; forging personal strength while each month's goal is realized.

During your two-year period of laying low and saving money (according to your RAW goal), you will find out if your partner is truly committed to the task, or if you are destined to go it alone. Either way, your daily, weekly, monthly, yearly, and overall goals need to come from you. Should a girlfriend or boyfriend wish to join you, make sure they are part of the solution and not a burden to be endured. Your two-year stint is to set goals, achieve them, develop self-discipline, learn a skill and establish good habits that will last a lifetime. Is your partner onboard?

Rule number four: Develop a marketable skill and expertise.

Laying low for two years is the time to learn. Determine what you are excited about and figure out if that field has opportunities to make money. Yes? That's great. If not, then it is time to cultivate knowledge that will make you an expert in another area. This is your second task... while laying low for two years, working at your mundane job and saving the majority of your measly paycheque; do everything in your power to learn about the area you wish to specialize in. Pick the minds of any people involved with what you wish to become accomplished at. Read everything you can lay your hands on: books, magazines and web sites. Your confidence and knowledge will grow. Before too long you will be able to separate fact from fiction, especially from internet sources.

You can never learn all there is to know about any subject; at least you will have a base of knowledge before you put your Deal Bag money to work. This is part of the transformation, building confidence through information and knowledge, then applying your expertise to make money... simple.

Developing a marketable skill is what happens when you enrol in college or university. As a blue-collar worker it is your responsibility to educate yourself. During your two years of laying low and saving money it is time to develop positive study habits. Evenings can be wasted playing video games or you can choose to better yourself by learning all there is to know about the field that interests you.

Nobody is going to force you to learn about your chosen field of interest; it should be your passion, you will want to do it because you love it. Whether it is vintage cars, art, motorbikes, rare books, antique furniture, collectible firearms, Chinese porcelain, comic books, sports memorabilia, vintage clothing: or any of a million other items related to what excites you. Find some passion that will engage and enthuse you for a lifetime. It will be a joy to dedicate time to something you love. Making money at it will be icing on the cake.

Vintage and collector cars are a huge market. The scope is so large a person can specialize in one of hundreds of niches. Cars, or their parts, can be sold to any corner of the world. Learning about cool cars and their values was central to my profitable deal-making for many years. Because I loved anything to do with vintage vehicles it was never work to me. If you don't have such a passion, now is the time to discover it and learn all you can about your new love. Then you can...

Rule number five: Start making deals.

You have taken the effort to educate yourself for two years. You know your area of expertise fairly well. A Deal Bag of money is waiting to be pressed into action. You have followed trends and know which direction the market for your item is heading. A specific set of goals and objectives has been laid out by you for dealing from a position of strength. Lowballing techniques and specifics of negotiating have been ingrained in your brain; time to start making deals (see later chapter on lowballing).

The temptation to hit a home run, go all in, or commit the entire contents of your Deal Bag in your first transaction may cause you to rush in and do something foolish. Do your homework. If the deal seems too good to be true you might be on the losing end of a con job. You've worked too hard and sacrificed too much to become a victim of your own over zealous enthusiasm for a deal by being blinded to red flags.

Do yourself a favour; start small. Build confidence, experience, knowledge and wisdom as you follow your specific steps and goals for each transaction. It can be quite thrilling to purchase a project, to count out thousands in crisp, hundred dollar bills, to quell your excitement in the negotiating phase and shake hands when a deal has been struck... but make sure you are on the winning side each time. Starting small and being familiar with the nuts and bolts of the process of buying low and selling high will become second nature the more it is practiced. If you do happen to lose on a few of your initial deals, at least it will be on a smaller scale and figuring out what you did wrong will be less costly.

Like any skill, practice makes perfect. Mechanics of making deals (sourcing, negotiating, adding value and reselling) are basically the same if you are playing with five hundred or fifty thousand dollars. Be patient and build confidence as you work into larger and more profitable transactions. That way you will always keep yourself on the winning side of most transactions, instead of being mad at yourself for losing money.

Rule number six: Deal from a position of strength.

As you start to buy and sell, you will meet people of various backgrounds, income levels, age, experience, intelligence, character and desperation: practically every variable of circumstance. One thing however, needs to remain constant — you.

When you enter a potential deal, numerous things need to be consistent: your goal, your money, your expertise, your negotiating ability, your option of leaving or proceeding with the deal and your confidence in controlling the situation. Dealing from a position of strength stems from preparation and having a plan. Knowing that you can walk away from any deal if the price isn't within your preset parameters is your greatest strength. Being aware that another deal of a similar nature exists and you're not cornered into buying a one of a kind item that may (or may not) have numerous buyers lined up to outbid you, is your other great strength. Some sellers are very savvy and experienced in pulling emotional strings that are connected to your Deal Bag. Not being caught up in an emotion–over–common sense moment (by being prepared) is your third strength.

Always approach any deal from a position of strength. Same holds true for the sale. You've done everything right (bought low, added value) and now it's time to sell for a profit. Are you desperate to sell because you are in a financial bind? Do you have to sell at a loss because you're terrible at managing money? Of course not. In fact, you have a wonderful item that you have improved and it is priced fairly. Should someone offer you a lowball amount you can thank them for their time and entertain the next offer. Sell from a position of strength.

This becomes habitual as you apply the parameters of your RAW goals to each deal. This is what will distinguish you from most buyers and sellers, an actual plan of attack before engaging in either side of a deal. And that is a position of strength.

Rule number seven: Never use Deal Bag money for living.

Savings that are set aside for deal making (your Deal Bag) are sacred. Not to be spent on anything but profitable ventures. Simplest of the ten rules... in theory. In practice, it can be one of the most difficult to maintain. Keeping a separate bank account for a large sum of money that is earmarked for profit-making deals while you live a frugal existence can be a challenge. Many temptations will come your way at every stage.

A couple months into your two-year plan of saving money should see you with two or three grand in the bank. Don't be surprised when a buddy from work hits you up for a loan. His truck needs a transmission, his girlfriend is pregnant and he's going to inherit ten grand when his ailing Aunt dies in a few months. He'll pull at your emotional connection, "Dude have a heart, just need three grand to get me over this rough patch. When my Aunt dies I'll pay you right back. It's just like money in the bank, you can't lose, and you'll be helping me and my ole' lady. Dude, we're friends, right?"

What to do? Find out if your friend is trying to take advantage, or respects you and your goals. Say something like, "I hope we're friends, that's why I told you my goal three months ago of living cheaply and saving a grand a month for two years. I hope you can respect that... and understand why I can't loan anyone my savings."

How would a true friend respond to such a statement? "Yeah, I can respect what you're trying to do."

Someone attempting to take advantage of you, that had no intention of paying you back might say, "And I thought we were friends! How can you be so cruel! My girlfriend is pregnant! How am I going to drive to work? It's only three grand! You know you'll get it back!"

Rest assured if your friend becomes angry, he's no friend; never has been, never will be. You just 'qualified' your workmate, dealt from a position of strength, commanded respect, held onto your money, re-established your goals, built confidence and stood your ground. Practice this. I can assure you, there will be more attempts and temptations to have you part with Deal Bag money.

Loved ones. Your girlfriend may have been alongside for a year, sharing a frugal lifestyle, pooling savings. Together you may have saved twenty-four thousand in twelve months. A major goal accomplished; congratulations. The two of you contemplate the future... making deals. One of you has a slightly different idea of how money should be invested.

"Honey, we've been living in your Granddad's basement for a year, doing all his yard work; it's been fun, but I feel it's time for us to rent our own place, and maybe furnish it. Wouldn't take much money. Bedroom suite, leather sofa, big-screen TV, we could furnish a nice little place for ten or twelve grand. We've got plenty. It would really be an investment in us."

I'll leave the reader to decide whether 'he' or 'she' might make such an appeal. Don't cave, don't use deal money for anything but profit-making. At a certain point in the future, when your life is sufficiently sorted and you are comfortable with dedicating resources to personal luxury, then you can break from character and spoil yourself. For now, you need to stick to your goals.

Try the same... can-you-respect-my-goals-speech with your teammate, if he or she insists that the best course of action is to spend (deal bag savings) to furnish an apartment, then it might be time to let her (or him) do just that. Parting ways (with half the savings going out the door) is best done at this early stage. Conversely, if he or she just had a temporary bout of light headedness, you can return to the business of sticking to your objectives.

Set goals together as to what that is; might be purchase of an apartment when seventy thousand dollars is in the Deal Bag, with ten grand of that dedicated to furnishings. Such decisions and goals stem from building a solid financial foundation, not from decimating your Deal Bag in the very beginning.

Giving in to temptation (wherever it comes from) to use money from your special account for anything but growth is a notion that has erosive tendencies. Careful consideration must also be given when that money is to be used for purchase of real estate. Is mortgage debt a good thing? Can you buy property without borrowing from a bank? Only you can answer such questions as your situation evolves.

Discipline to stay the course and stick to your goals will command respect, it will help determine who amongst your workmates, family, and loved ones, are with you or... not.

By establishing RAW goals and doing your best to live according to your self-imposed course of improvement will attract certain types, leading to the next rule.

Rule number eight: Align yourself with like-minded people.

People can drag you down or build you up; it is in your best interest to be with those persons who complement what you are trying to achieve. Girlfriend, workmates, family; doesn't matter how you are associated with an individual or group, just ask yourself one question, "Is he (or she) a problem or a solution?"

When you take the time to step back and examine the people in your life, it can be a revelation. Often we are blinded to a person's influence simply because they have been around for many years. A parent, a boss, boyfriend, wife; there might be someone (and their demands of time) that has a detrimental impact in your life. Because that certain person has been a factor for a length of time, their presence has become the norm. Perhaps it's difficult to see the forest for the trees, but when you do, it's time to do something about it.

Aligning yourself with the right people is similar to being on a winning team. The choice is yours. Struggle with losers, or make life better by surrounding yourself with like-minded people who are aiming for similar results. Sounds simple. Yet, how do you distance yourself from a needy, widowed parent that requires constant care and attention?

How do you tell your girlfriend/boyfriend/husband/wife that they need to get on board with a new game plan or they are cut from the team? How do you tell your old Sunday school teacher (that has called on you over the years to help out with every cause) that you need to dedicate time to your other interests and goals?

It starts by informing people of your goals, followed by seeking to align yourself with others who share similar objectives. As soon as you reveal your RAW goals to a person (that has been less than a team player) you will receive a reaction. Might be positive or it might be less than enthusiastic. A person's basic character usually won't change just because you have decided to improve your life by sharing your goals with them.

Either way, you'll quickly determine if a problematic person will adjust his or her actions to become more of a solution. If not, you need to make some changes. Only you can balance the fine line of your situation and seek to lessen the time you dedicate to the "problem" makers.

Working and associating with solution makers is far more productive. No situation in life is perfect, same with people; we all have our strengths and weaknesses of character. Just knowing what you are not so good at will assist you in aligning yourself with people that can fill a void. Any team will have individuals that are better at certain skills. Making all players work toward a winning situation is the key. That is your job: assemble a winning team. It may be just you and your partner. It might be three employees that form part of your little business as you move from minimum wage earner to business owner while the group of you pursue a common passion.

No situation in life is ideal, striving for excellence is about all any of us can do, achieving a level of success with your goals will come a lot easier when you take the time to align with team players who are interested in winning.

In the "People" section will be examples of success and failure. Most success stories are of proper alignment between like-minded individuals. More often than not they also work in cooperation with large movements in the economy. Which leads to the next rule.

Rule number nine: "Take advantage of macro economics."

The big picture. Being in the right place at the right time has been the major reason many people became wealthy. Most self-made wealthy people are no smarter than you or I, they just happened to be surrounded by an abundance of opportunity... and they were wise enough to milk it while they could.

As economies expand and contract on an international stage, there will be consequences; positive and negative. Being smart enough to see major trends in markets means you can take advantage of growing or shrinking activity in your local market as it is affected by global affairs. Not only can you profit from buoyant economic conditions (when you know how the trend is unfolding) but you can profit from advanced knowledge of an "easy-credit-bubble about to burst" and realize even greater gains. It stems from being informed.

Knowing what fiscal planners are doing at the Federal Reserve regarding interest rates, money printing, manipulation of stock markets, commodity price-fixing-collusion and a host of other parameters regarding their hand in affecting the world of business is a good starting point.

What effect do policy makers in major economic power houses around the world have on your situation? Central banks in Europe, China, Japan and the United States constantly wage currency wars with one another; alliances can switch, with consequences that trickle down to common workers in many parts of the world. Having some knowledge of macroeconomics provides you with insight to profit from your local (micro) economy.

You don't need to have a degree in economics to know whether prices for basic goods are rising (inflation) or falling (deflation). In fact, most bona fide economists with multiple degrees from Ivy league universities are notoriously poor at predicting future trends in economic activity. Often it's a "can't see the trees for the forest" type of confusion that muddles most economists' thinking.

As volatile swings in global alliances bring about changes in economic activity you can be ready to pounce on opportunities with reserves of cash and knowledge. Example: United States slaps sanctions on Russia for expanding into Ukraine, Soviet Union creates a "work around" and sells more of their petroleum to China. They accept rubles, renminbi or gold instead of U.S. dollars for payment. Saudi Arabia doesn't like the fact that one of their big customers (China) is buying more oil from Russia, they can't easily cut back on their own production of oil; now the Saudis' have a glut of the stuff. More supply than demand means prices fall. In a few months of this action, the cost of gasoline at your pump is cut by forty percent. How do you profit from such a price war? Can you? Does any of this affect business activity in your city, state, province or county? Is it possible to be informed enough to take advantage of such a domino effect of world events?

I believe it is possible. Further information regarding macroeconomic activity and how to inform yourself in order to profit from said knowledge is found in the addendum of this book.

Rule number ten: "Don't quit your day job until you are ready."

Not everyone is cut out to be self-employed. Only you can decide that, like every stage of development or change that transpires in your life, it needs to be approached from a position of strength. Quitting your minimum wage job before you have sufficient confidence to be your own boss can sometimes result in a giant step backwards. There is a huge difference between cocky and confident. The cocky person usually fails because he lacks real expertise and seeks to mask his shortcomings through big talk, with no substance to back his brash claims. Quiet confidence is the better route to success, that and building a business on a sound, debt-free foundation.

Starting small and establishing credibility, a customer base, and providing a quality product at a fair price is a superior plan that will have a far greater chance of long-term success. Jumping into the deep end of a business with borrowed money puts tremendous pressure on the boss to concentrate on keeping ahead of the debt's repayment. Such a position of weakness can be a motivator, but (more often than not) focusing on the monthly payment makes bad decisions more common. Most small businesses fail because they started with debt and enthusiastic owners who weren't quite ready to deal from a position of strength.

Numerous business ventures have started from a room in a house or a garage, slowly evolving into bona fide enterprises as customers and income are established. When the return for your effort is greater than your paycheque from your minimum wage job, then you should consider making the leap to being self-employed.

Examples of success and failure are given in the 'People' section that illustrate how the transition from minimum wage employee to wealthy business owner is possible; avoiding the pitfalls of quitting your day job too soon and incurring unnecessary losses.

Chapter Three

People

Human beings are constantly dealing with each other, nothing has really changed in the human condition on a fundamental level. Your ability to observe the machinations of mankind on a large and small scale, then positively applying what has transpired into a worthwhile lesson (that serves to improve your life) is what separates the wise student from the rest.

Each person you work with presents many opportunities to see how problems are solved, or not. Being exposed to many people over the course of a varied career can be a valuable education. It has been just that for myself. The distillation of the ten rules that comprise "Blue-Collar Riches" is the result of working with/for/alongside many people from around the world... far too many to fit within the confines of a single book. Observing friends, roommates, family and neighbours go about the business of life can be added to the cumulative knowledge of what you learn from workmates.

Your ability to step back and decipher the observations and questions you ask yourself about a person's success or failure will be helpful. Not repeating a friend or work-mate's mistakes is what will add to your knowledge. As

you read about the people in this section (that I have had direct experience with) try to overlay the ten rules of "Blue-Collar Riches" and see where each person displayed strength, weakness, success or failure.

Review:

1. Set and achieve RAW goals.

2. Live as cheap as possible for two years.

3. Save as much money as possible.

4. Develop a marketable skill and expertise.

5. Start making deals.

6. Deal from a position of strength.

7. Never use Deal Bag for living.

8. Align yourself with like-minded people.

9. Take advantage of macroeconomics.

10. Don't quit your day job till you are ready.

How could the people you will read about have improved their situation? Were they lucky? Skilled? Did they have talent? Intelligence? Perseverance? Did they have a plan? Goals?

Some accounts of peoples' lives will have more detail than others; rest assured, each person I've written about could have two or three chapters dedicated to them. All the people are real, numerous have passed on, while others are actively building their positions of wealth.

Open yourself to the notion that every person, no matter how humble, arrogant or wise, can teach something; just have to look for it. Might be a good habit, an idea, an attitude, a philosophy or insights into specific markets. Maybe their constant mistakes will be your take away. Doesn't matter what it is. Your powers of observation in assessing people and those you choose to align with will shape your future... for better or worse.

In no particular order, but starting with one of the youngest, I will introduce a few of the people that I have associated with in numerous decades and their lessons.

Jay; a young man (twenty-one) that went from indebted to fairly successful. Circumstance and an ability to find a passion played vital roles in his story.

Five of us young men rented a hundred-year-old house in North Burnaby (B.C., Canada); it had seen better days. Three of us were the core, long-term group that occupied the tired edifice. Two hundred dollars a month (each) was affordable. Seemed we were looking for a new roommate every few months. Maybe it was us. Jay came to us via word of mouth. Paul was moving out to marry Jay's sister. Jay was moving to the west coast from Toronto. His sister's wedding would fit nicely into the grand scheme. Sliding into his future brother in-law's room would serve all our needs.

Young Jay arrived with baggage. Drove cross-country in an old Ford van that was a decommissioned ambulance. It was a little rough; fit in perfect with the decor. For the journey, Jay was armed with his trusty Canadian Tire credit card. His father owned a large and successful Canadian Tire franchise in Toronto. Jay spent countless hours in formative years working at the store. Being groomed to follow in father's footsteps was not Jay's idea of a good time. He headed west to find himself. Jay, with his parents' blessing, was going to be a helicopter pilot.

West Coast Helicopters offered an intense course of study that practically ensured its graduates would be employed somewhere in the industry. Cost? Twenty-thousand (early 1990s) dollars. Jay's parents agreed to pay the tuition. Only one condition: Jay was responsible to pay for everything else once he arrived in Vancouver. Slight problem; young Jay didn't have a dime to his name. Partied it away in Toronto. He was very familiar with that city's nightclubs.

Without a dollar to his name Jay convinced a friend to drive across Canada with him. Paid for half the gas; said cash went into Jay's wallet while Jay used his Canadian Tire charge card to purchase gasoline and junk food. They fuelled the van (and their bellies) on Dad's tab as they stopped at Canadian Tire gas bars on the cross-country trek.

Jay (and his van loaded with chips, pop and chocolate bars) made it to Vancouver, he said goodbye to his friend and moved into our house as the latest roommate. Two hundred dollars (of gas money) in his pocket covered a month's rent. Perfect.

Happy-go-lucky Jay embarked on his west coast adventure with a plan; any shortfall in cash would soon be a thing of the past as he had every intention of winning the lottery. His personal credit card was nearing its limit of a few thousand, most of his charges were for cash advances. Cash that he used to purchase lottery tickets: hundreds of them. Jay had convinced himself he was a winner. Was only a matter of 'when' he would strike it big. He knew he was lucky, it was in his genes.

Jay's uncle won eight million dollars in one of Canada's earliest (late 1970s) government-sanctioned lotteries. Jay was a ten-year-old at the time. This event had many spin-offs (more on those later), one of which was to convince young Jay that he would be a winner like his uncle. Just needed to keep buying tickets. Work for a living? That's for losers, Jay was a winner. If he had to work, it would be as a cool helicopter pilot. Until, of course, he won the Big One.

Six months and twenty thousand dollars of parents' money later, Jay graduated from helicopter school with a pilot's license in hand. There were jobs waiting for him up north. How far north? Arctic Circle. Seismic crews, mining companies, oil and gas outfits; they all needed pilots. Rookie pilots with few hours in their logbooks were needed immediately for high-paying, dangerous jobs. Only one problem: Jay had no intention (nor desire) to pilot a chopper in the frozen environment of the high-north. Besides, he was going to win the lottery. All of his problems would be solved.

During his six months of attending pilot school, Jay managed to earn a few dollars cleaning windows. With supplies purchased from Canadian Tire he would clean windows of two or three houses each month to pay his minimal bills and credit card interest. Meanwhile, his enthusiasm for all things 'helicopter' were fading at the same rate as his chances of winning the Big One.

Convincing his mother how endangered his young life would be by accepting a job near the North Pole was easy; took a bit more effort to sway dad to bankroll his next passion: broadcasting. Radio jock, that's what Jay wanted to be. Course of study cost twelve-thousand dollars. Jay sold his parents on the safer career of being the next Golden Voice.

Months of broadcasting courses had Jay squeaking by, trying to pay rent and feed himself. Window washing was quickly losing its appeal and his roommates endured a constant barrage of the on-air-voice. Jay's joy at learning to be a highly paid and adored radio personality was waning as he lost patience with his instructors; they just didn't appreciate the fact he should be on the air right now. Our young student wanted quicker gratification; like winning the lottery, his life wasn't happening instantly. Life was piling up around Jay; chipping away at his spirit.

Trying to self-medicate with as much binge-drinking as his meagre finances permitted had Jay convinced he needed to augment his tiny amount of window washing income with a real paycheque. What to do?

Numerous part time jobs were available for anyone willing to work. Jay wanted something easy. A job that would pay well but didn't ask too much in effort, either physical or mental. The Keg Steak House needed numerous positions filled at most of their locations: busboys, dishwashers, waitstaff, bartenders and managers. Willing hands were needed to join their winning team.

Jay went to the steak house with the idea of being a superstar bartender. Downtown store hired him and he started the next day. Not as a highly paid 'tender of the bar', as a minimum wage waiter... a waiter in training.

Menial job that paid minimum wage (plus tips) was intended to help Jay pay his bills while he attended broadcasting school, en route to his vocation as 'DJ Jay, the Man with the Golden Tonsils'. Funny thing happened. Jay loved being part of his new team. Wasn't very long till he dropped out of school (full tuition paid in advance) and joined his new friends in the food industry on a full-time basis.

Our young man found a passion he never knew existed. No situation is perfect but Jay found very little to complain about in his new career. Camaraderie, witty banter, cash tips, food, format of rating/evaluating/reward/praise, after hours socializing and cute waitresses were part of the allure. Working full-time, found Jay ahead of his bills in short order.

A few months into The Keg groove had Jay enthused about life. Work was more fun than laborious and it showed in Jay's joy. With his keen mind, good looks, easy-going charm and ability to up-sell most customers into gladly spending more money than they had intended, Jay advanced quickly. Jay had genuine joy for his work and was soon the head server all the newbies looked to for advice on being number one.

We all expected Jay to hit a wall; lose interest in his career as a waiter and switch teams. Week after week, Jay went to work. Good times on the job outweighed the bad, by a large margin. Jay kept smiling and looked forward to his next day of teamwork. Confidence oozed from Jay as he was praised by management for his constant ability to be at the top of the heap of money earners.

Growing up in a retail environment where he saw his father deal with customers (using charm and grace) was paying off. Jay's brain wasn't idle, he noted similarities and glaring differences between the two retail chains. Canadian Tire and The Keg were both concerned with consistency and customer satisfaction. One offered food-stuffs, the other; consumer goods.

An ability to steer a cantankerous customer into a smiling tipper (with a well-placed piece of chocolate-sauce-slathered-gratis-cheesecake and a sincere apology for an imagined wrong) was part of what gave Jay an advantage over his fellow servers. He was good at his job. A job he loved. A job in an industry with many career paths.

Time for a tangent. We'll leave Jay for a moment and tell his uncle's story. You remember... the lucky winner of eight million dollars.

Uncle Peter, like the rest of Jay's clan; good-looking, charming, well-spoken, intelligent and middle-class... what most people would consider as a success. True, he had won millions. Not a small amount of money. I met Peter and received his story in person.

With his cheque of many millions in hand, an elated Peter and his young wife looked forward to the good life. They knew instant riches would bring with it certain obstacles: long-lost friends, con artists, aggressive charities, relatives and any number of people with their hands out looking for a bit of the easy money. Fending off petty hucksters turned out to be simple. That was the least of Peter's troubles.

With a young family of two toddlers and a small but growing business, Pete and his wife felt confident about the future. Peter had started a business with a lifelong friend a few years before. The two men developed a technique of constructing large, fake-rock structures out of sprayed fibre-glass. The type of rocky outcrop you'd see at a zoo with gorillas clambering on it. Business was good. Partner and Pete kept themselves busy finding new clients, developing machinery, maintaining existing instalments and making sure their Toronto-based business kept ahead of expenses.

Peter floated back to work on a cloud of lottery-winning-elation, for a few days it was business as usual. Partner and their two employees had a celebration; all smiles. Lucky Peter and his partner (lifelong friend) kicked around a few ideas about the future, how things were going to be bright. Didn't take long for the future to land on Pete.

Partner's lawyer initiated a lawsuit. Goal? Half the winnings. Peter consulted and hired a law firm for their advice. There were a lot of questions. Very few solid answers. This could take a while. Lawyers lined up on both sides. Fight was on. Peter's problems of a legal nature took over his life. Business was put on hold. Peter said, "I won the money. It's mine!" His partner, "Everything fifty- fifty!"

Lawyers on both sides found many legal arguments that cost time and money. This was the 1970s; government-sponsored and sanctioned gambling was in its infancy. Legal wrangling lasted five years. Amount of money Peter expended on his legal team went from a nibbling amount on the interest to great hunks bitten out of the principal.

Verdict was finally in. Court found in favour of the plaintiff. Peter lost the case; ordered to pay his partner half the winnings, plus five-years of interest. He could appeal to a higher court. Why? His fight was done. He knew where he stood and didn't want to pay lawyers another dollar. Stress of five years had taken a toll. Heated arguments with his wife nearly ended their marriage (another partner fight?). Family and friends, with their constant advice and petty runs at the money had kept Pete wary, weary and stressed for years. Time to move on.

Certified cheque of four million, plus interest, was paid to his partner's legal team. With the dust settled, Pete was left with a little under two million dollars, no partner, and a withered business that built fake-rock installations. He breathed a sigh of relief.

As I conversed with Jay's Uncle, this was all in the past, over a decade from the settlement. Since then he had thrown himself with renewed vigour into his business. As a sole proprietor he called all the shots and business flourished. Family life was good. One of his sons was enthused about working alongside his father.

Asked him if he had any regrets from the whole affair, Peter said "Yes, just one, buying a lottery ticket." Hasn't bought one since. His final word on the subject, "You can't lose if you don't play."

What Jay saw as a youngster was a lucky Uncle that had the world by its tail. His cousins lived in a bigger house, played with the latest toys, while Jay had to work at Canadian Tire on Saturdays to earn an allowance. If only he could tap into some of that Loto Magic.

Jay was now a man in his early twenties. Starting to learn that money didn't appear magically, it had to be managed, not wished for.

The steakhouse offered ample opportunity for advancement; Jay flourished in the freewheeling, yet structured world of a large corporation. Young men of sound character were being groomed to progress from servers to managers; Jay was showing his ability by performing above his job-description as a super-waiter by training, encouraging, scheduling and team-building with others. A weeklong management course was offered to Jay. He had been with the steakhouse for over a year; seasoned server. Jay had filled in at various locations and was respected by busboys and bosses everywhere, he jumped at the chance to be one of the leaders.

Young Jay proved to be an enthusiastic student and excelled at any and all aspects during his week of intense study. His seven days of school was conducted at head office in Toronto. Old stomping grounds had Jay wishing he was back in Ontario. When Jay returned to Vancouver he applied for a transfer to the first available assistant-manager position that would come up in his beloved Toronto.

Didn't take long. Jay accepted an opening about a month after his training. On his way back to Toronto. He had a couple of years of finding himself and wasn't the same kid that came west. Jay had a few dollars to his name, no debt, a passion for his job and a new motorbike underneath his butt. Time for another adventure: drive across Canada on a motor-cycle. What could go wrong?

Jay settled into his role as assistant-manager with ease. Loved by all. An ability to sniff out new suppli-ers and increase profit at his store was noticed by head office. He could rally and train his staff and command their loyalty by being a great boss. After-hours parties were the stuff of legend as Jay bonded with his team. On top of the world, that's what he was.

Then it happened... in the middle of the day. They claimed not to have seen a thing. A car, stuffed full of recently arrived immigrants from Eastern Europe (that barely spoke English) decided to pull a U-turn in the middle of a four-lane bridge. Jay, on his mo-torbike, was traveling behind them at highway speed when the sudden maneuver happened. Rammed into the side of the vehicle and flew over the roof. Woke up in the hospital. Worst of his injuries was a leg. The left required multiple pins and operations to mend numerous fractures.

Three months later Jay hobbled out of the hospital on crutches. Benefits from work saw to it that he received a good percentage of his wage (bills could be paid) and regular visits from workmates and family kept his spirits up. Jay was still enthused about work and looked forward to being part of his team again.

A few more months of therapy and recovery; Jay was back at work. He couldn't hustle like he did as a superstar server, but in his management position, he didn't need to. During his months of downtime Jay had ample opportunity to think. He came to the same conclusion constantly; he liked his job, it was his passion, he had found what he was good at. Work was fun, it wasn't a burden to be endured. Jay had found himself.

One year after his accident and well on his way to a full recovery, Jay was now the manager of his steakhouse; a respected boss. Time for a bonus. His insurance company had settled the lawsuit against the insurance company that represented the carload of U-turning immigrants. Result: a cheque of three-hundred thousand dollars. Compensation for his injuries. What to do with his windfall? Jay knew that he was passionate about managing restaurants. Time to establish roots. Toronto was his birthplace, somehow it represented the past... and a certain amount of pain. Vancouver represented the future. Jay headed west again. Not on a motorbike.

Back in Vancouver, money in the bank, skills and experience in hand. Glowing recommendation from Toronto bosses, future; bright. New job as senior manager of a successful Irish pub/restaurant/night-club secured. Jay in his mid twenties, confidently went about the task of life.

Jay gave me a call. We met at the Irish pub he was boss of; talked in his office. Topic? Money.

Since first knowing Jay I was one of few people that talked with him about managing money. About set-ting goals, making budgets; how to stick to them and avoid silly traps like taking cash-advances on credit cards to buy lottery tickets. We both laughed as Jay proudly stated he hadn't paid any interest on his credit cards in the last few years nor had he purchased a lottery ticket. Young Jay had come a long way in a short time.

With a few hundred thousand (1990s dollars) in the bank, Jay sought the advice of a few people he respected when it came to monetary matters. My advice was to purchase a place to live; in a decent neighbourhood. Then establish a budget that would allow a set percentage of his monthly pay to be invested. Did not provide him with specific details as to what he should put money towards, only that any investment should be a comfortable reflection of the amount of risk/reward he was willing to live with.

Few weeks later Jay purchased an apartment in a well-built high-rise not too far from his place of employment. Paid in full, no mortgage. Took most of his money in the bank to do it but Jay was very happy with the transaction.

As he slowly transformed the Irish pub into a more profitable enterprise, he took months to educate himself on investment possibilities.

Where is Jay now? Twenty (plus) years later he is a successful owner/operator of a large pub/restaurant/bar in the heart of Vancouver, British Columbia, Canada. He is also a proud father (of one daughter) and mentor to many young men and women that find themselves lucky enough to be employed at his establishment. A portfolio of sound investments (that continually return a steady stream of profit) is just one more feather in Jay's cap that he can be proud of.

What did I learn from Jay? What can you learn from his experience? First: no matter how young you are (or old), you have the ability to be stupid with money, or smart. Learning how to make money work in your favour isn't too difficult. One key is to find your passion. Once you have done that; stick to it. Most people go to work every day and hate their job, they then extend that stress to their home, family and life.

Jay bounced from wanting to be a helicopter pilot to radio personality; neither vocation ignited a real passion in him. He might be a miserable and stressed helicopter pilot had he continued on that route. Almost by accident he stumbled into his life's passion. You can as well. Time to bounce from minimum wage jobs is when you are young. Never know which industry or sector of the economy is going to excite you. Might find your passion. I can tell you from experience, there are many opportunities to buy-low, sell-high in every minimum wage related job. We'll deal with that in later chapters.

I learned from Jay and his Uncle Peter that pinning your hopes on winning the lottery is a fool's game. You are better served by learning how to manage money and being in control of your financial future. Should a lump sum of money land in your lap, as it did in Jay's case via an accident settlement, you are prepared to deal with it. Imagine twenty-one year-old Jay with the three hundred grand; he would have blown half of it playing the big shot at night-clubs, buying rounds of drinks and trying too hard to impress. Thousands would have been spent on lottery tickets; maybe he could have won big... probability of that happening is billions of times against the player.

Would Jay be in his sound financial position without his insurance settlement? I think he would. He had established numerous habits that stemmed from following his passion of being part of the food service industry. Good habits of becoming a fine manager of people and money through setting budgets, goals, living frugally, working with a passion and sticking to it. Jay did it, so can you.

Next person I will introduce started like Jay; a young man with no particular plan, goals or defined passion. Very little to his name, not even a credit card. John's story began at the end of World War Two, when credit cards didn't exist, the late 1940s.

Born in Palm Springs, California in the 1920s, John was of a generation that war affected. To that end he volunteered to serve in Uncle Sam's army during the war. Displaying enough intelligence to be assigned to officer training proved acceptable to John and he was hustled off to join other candidates in various classrooms. Before he could be sent into battle as a leader of men, the war ended. John could stay with the military and make a career of it or take his discharge, rejoining the world as a civilian. Our young man had seen enough of military life to know he shared no enthusiasm for wearing a uniform.

John returned to his hometown east of Los Angeles. Palm Springs in the 1940s was barely a speck on a map. These were the days before freeways crisscrossed the Los Angeles basin; before millions of vehicles and people created gridlock on a daily basis. These were slower times, but things were changing...

Word was out, soldiers from many states had compared notes with each other during the war. General consensus; California is where you ought to be. Movement was on, people that is, sun and opportunity was pulling them to the Golden State like a magnet.

John found ample work in his tiny town of Palm Springs. He joined a small construction crew that built homes. Palm Springs was growing. In short order John became skilled at most aspects of residential construction. He liked it. Before long his tanned, good looks were noticed by one of the local gals. The young couple were married within a few weeks. "That's how it happened in the '40s," John assured me.

A wife and the prospect of small mouths to feed meant John was responsible for others. He went to his local bank to apply for a mortgage. Sufficient funds to purchase a serviced lot and build a modest house were requested. John had a job, a small down payment, and he and his family were well-known by the loan officer. Funding was secured. With help from workmates and friends, John toiled after regular hours and weekends to put a roof over their heads. It was a struggle to make payments and feed themselves but John felt the sacrifice would someday be worth it.

Palm Springs wasn't the sleepy community John had grown up in; things were happening. Post war boom was on, how far things could grow was anybody's guess. John received a clue one day.

Relaxing with his wife after supper, there was a knock at the door; well-dressed man greeted John and complimented him and the missus on their lovely new home. Next question out of his mouth, "Would you like to sell your house?"

Didn't take a genius to make a decision. John was propositioned by a real estate broker who offered a fair amount of money for the (mostly) finished house. He informed John there existed more customers than he could find homes for. John had a little battle convincing his wife that it was time to move, but no problem with his bank-manager when he paid off his mortgage and reapplied for enough funds to build two houses. One for the missus and the other to be sold.

Supply and demand were dynamics that John could see in front of his eyes. His house was worth seven thousand dollars yet it sold for eighty-five hundred. "That fifteen hundred dollars represented the income of a year swinging a hammer. In 1948 that was huge money," John relived the emotion of his first house deal with relish, even though it had transpired many years before.

John saw an opportunity and started his own business. He was now a home builder. Rising economic activity meant he was in the right place at the right time. Prices of houses were going up faster than the cost of building them. John also showed a profit on the sale of his second home. His young wife was happy with the larger home they moved into on the same street.

John's company grew rapidly. Four houses were soon under construction with his young crew and himself. Sold. Try eight houses. Sold. Before John knew what had happened, twenty years had passed, three sons were born and his company 'Race Setter Homes' were developing entire subdivisions, hundreds of homes at a time in Los Angeles county and south into Orange county. Communities of Corona, Corona Del Mar, Hawthorne, Anaheim, Irvine, Riverside; some of the areas in southern California where John constructed thousands of homes.

He formed other companies as potential for profit and complementary businesses kept his operations flowing smoothly. John built the roads, sewers, sidewalks, play-grounds, shopping centres and other infrastructure that his new communities needed. Even owned a modest string of banks to help his customers purchase Race Setter houses. John was the sole proprietor of one of the largest home development companies in California. A millionaire many times over, yet very humble and approachable.

A few years into his career as a developer, John started to reap handsome rewards in the form of profit. Still in his prime of physical and mental health, John decided to indulge a passion besides building homes: race cars. 1960s California was (and still is) a mecca for speed-freaks of all sorts, hot rodders, drag racers, dry lakes racers and sports car aficionados were a small sample of the gear-heads that flocked to California in record numbers. John was in the thick of it; purchased and drove many sports cars from the muscle era. Sponsored numerous race cars and teams, including an Indy car that allowed him a prominent rolling billboard to ensure Race Setter Homes was seen by many. John rubbed shoulders with many of the famous racers of the era: Carroll Shelby, Mark Donohue, Dickie Smothers, James Garner, Lance Revantlow, Parnelli Jones, Paul Newman, Steve McQueen, Chuck Daigh, Dan Gurney... some of the men that knew John on a first name basis. He had stories about them all.

Behind the wheel of a high powered race car, John displayed some talent at driving. He knew, compared to his professional friends he wasn't in the same league. This didn't hamper him from an expensive hobby of amateur club racing. Sports cars; from Cobras to Porsches were part of his stable for many years. That is how I came to know John, I was one of the two-man crew that worked full-time to maintain his small collection of cars.

Mid 1980s, Costa Mesa, California; John was a successful entrepreneur in his late sixties and I, an enthusiastic kid in my mid twenties.

Back to John's story. Massive growth in southern California's population from the late 1940s till the end of John's career in the late 1980s, meant just about anything John touched turned to gold. From pioneering 'storage unit' buildings to hiring the best people and paying them more than his competition to insure they were loyal and productive were just a few things that I learned from John (by asking him dozens of questions on our race weekends). In John's humble way he would say, on more than one occasion, "In all honesty Monty, it's not as though I was any smarter or more talented than anybody else, I was merely in the right place at the right time. Imagine trying to make a subdivision in rural Idaho of a thousand homes, you'd be broke before you started!"

John downplayed his intelligence and ability, I read between the lines how his applied level of expertise in his field of home-building kept him in profits and ahead of his competitors. He hated unions and saw them as the potential downfall of the entire nation. How their antagonistic 'take more, give less' attitude had infected an entire generation of workers. The age of entitlement where a unionized workforce could hold any industry in limbo while they demanded more rubbed John the wrong way. His strong opinion on the matter was based on first-hand experience as an employer of thousands.

Every one of John's companies was owned by him. No partners and no shareholders. Any employee could be fired for wrongdoing, thievery or sloth.

John's policy of paying more than the norm had people clambering to work for Race Setter Homes or any of his numerous ventures. His empire was international. An electronics factory in South Africa sold components for radios and televisions to name-brand manufacturers around the world. There were business concerns in Australia and numerous other states in the union that he paid top dollar to managers to see that profits kept rolling in. John employed thousands, including pilot and crew for his jet that was continually ferrying him around the world to make sure business was being conducted to a certain standard.

On the home front, John had three sons from his first marriage. All had graduated from the best universities and training. One was a fighter pilot with the Navy that flew from aircraft carriers. Two others were business majors. Oldest boy worked alongside dad at Race Setter Homes. Like his father, level-headed and humble. John, in his late sixties was on his first of two hip replacements and his fifth wife. "That's what you do Monty, you marry them." His latest partner was many years his junior and quite easy on the eyes.

John was still interested in fast cars (and women). He enjoyed life to the max. Latest wife knew how the game was played; as long as she didn't rock the boat, a red carpet of luxury was her's to be had. I took delight in occasionally calling John's personal secretary at Race Setter's office just to find out where he was, because we were friends she would say something quietly into the phone, "I'm not supposed to say... but he flew to Paris this morning with his wife to do a bit of shopping, oh, and there is some sort of car race in Monte Carlo they might catch."

What can be learned from John's life? How do any of his experiences relate to the rules of Blue-Collar Riches?

As admitted by John, he was in the right place at the right time and saw an opportunity when it knocked on his door. Imagine how different his life would have been had he not sold his first house... If he stuck to his first job as a construction labourer... if he listened to his first wife and stayed in Palm

Springs in their little 1940s bungalow. John was smart enough to see what was happening locally and nationally, he couldn't know how far into the future economic growth would extend, just that he had to take advantage of it while he could. John had four decades of being in the right place.

A young man earning a minimal wage as a construction labourer transformed his situation into maximum wealth by sacrifice, having goals, applying expertise, aligning himself with like-minded people and persevering. John's life was a great example of building riches from a humble beginning.

I was a young man in my twenties when I met and worked for John, basically the same age he was when he sold his first house. Could I have replicated his career and amount of success? Probably not; even John admitted he was lucky to have been in the situation where population growth in California continued for decades. I reminded him he was smart enough to recognize the situation. Humble as always, he simply nodded his head in agreement. John, with his immense riches and accomplishments of a successful life, could have been an arrogant, abrasive man... he wasn't. Quietly, confidently; John worked and did many deals from a position of strength.

What became of John? In his early seventies he quietly passed away; fifth wife at his side. John led a full life. Self-made man that passed his extensive legacy to his sons and their families. That's another story.

There were many people like John that I met during my time in southern California. Men that were able to build wealth from humble, blue-collar beginnings. Let's look at another and see what we can learn.

I met Les at Riverside Raceway during a race weekend in the mid 1980s. Like John, Les was a gentleman racer; an amateur that enjoyed piloting one (or more) of his collection of Ford and Porsche race cars. His stable of twenty (rare and valuable) automobiles and how he came to afford a collection that valued to many millions is an interesting story.

Similar to John, Les was born and raised in southern California, about ten years younger than his friend, Les was a product of the 1930s. While John, as a

young man, earned a living as a carpenter/construc-
tion labourer, Les was a plumber. Another blue-collar worker, a humble plumber that became a multi-
millionaire. How did he do it? Les saw an opportunity and jumped on it.

As a youngster, Les worked with his uncle and ap-
prenticed to be a plumber. Eventually Les had
enough experience with his uncle's plumbing company to strike out on his own. As a journeyman (and
with a co-signed loan from his uncle) Les purchased
his own tools and truck. He was in business as a
plumber; making the transition from minimum
wage apprentice to boss of his own company. Work
was plentiful in Los Angeles in the 1950s. Houses
were being built everywhere; Les quickly paid off his
loan and decided to expand his operation. There was
enough work for Les to operate two trucks and hire
another crew. Les had more ambition, energy and
enthusiasm than his elderly uncle, who was quite
content with his operation of one truck and special-
izing in residential plumbing.

Plenty of growth through the 1960s saw Les and his
plumbing business expanding into commercial

buildings while a fleet of a dozen trucks outfitted with the latest equipment was part of his empire. Plastic tubing that could be glued together came into use; Les and his workers learned how to quickly install profit making PVC systems. Profits rolled in.

More apartment buildings sprang up as developers saw the need to pack more people into each block. Les and his workers adapted accordingly. Buying material in bulk meant Les could realize more profit on large apartment jobs; paying to store the material ate away at that profit. Deciding to buy a large industrial lot to store his own material made economic sense. Les could see there was plenty of potential for growth as California welcomed more people to its sunny cities.

With a mortgage from his bank, Les bought a large lot and erected a Quonset to store plumbing supplies. Secure fencing meant his fleet of trucks had ample overnight parking. Racks of industrial pipe and tubing occupied a fair portion of the lot. There was no intention to sell supplies to other plumbers but before Les knew it, he was hanging around his storage building each morning as other plumbers arrived to purchase material. He hired a few older plumbers that knew the business and opened a retail/wholesale store to cater to all the demand. More profit rolled in. His store quickly became the go to place for anything to do with plumbing.

Les had to expand to keep pace with demand or stay the same size and be content with his situation. Our young plumber/entrepreneur/blue-collar worker decided to grow. Purchased more industrial lots; made two of his neighbours offers they found hard to resist. Les tripled in size overnight and moved the plumbing store out of the Quonset hut to a proper building next door. Expansion happened at a rapid pace; Les made sure he could afford each phase by having ample funds in the bank.

Technology in the field of plumbing isn't something that most people link with anything as lofty as space exploration, yet Les always looked for an edge to keep him ahead of the competition; this was the 1960s... there was talk of people landing on the moon. Les heard rumour of a simplified (on-off) fire-suppression system that might be incorporated into a building's plumbing, if the rumour were true, Les wanted in.

A few days of phoning friends, acquaintances and suppliers yielded a name. Les wasted no time in calling. The east coast company was owned by one man; a plumber. Les and his contact had many things in common, both were successful plumbers of similar age and interests. They talked at great length and realized that they might be able to align with each other in a profitable manner. It was true; his new friend had developed a sprinkler valve with on/off capability. It would allow water or fire retardant liquid to rain onto flames, then stop the flow of water; reducing water damage to buildings and contents. Both knew there was huge potential for the life saving system in the future of plumbing.

Les was on a flight the next day to the east coast where the two plumbers met. There were many topics to discuss. Who would buy a fire-suppression system? What was their market? What would the system cost? How would you sell it? How to maintain it? They talked into the night.

Next day the two men shook hands; Les presented his new friend (and business associate) with a cheque of a few thousand dollars to secure the west coast rights to the new sprinkler system. At this point, not one of the modern valves had been installed in any public or private building. Les was gambling on the technology, he had a gut feeling his investment was solid.

Took a few years to establish but when demand for the life saving fire-suppression sprinkler system took hold, Les was ready. He hit the ground running. Any installation west of the Rocky Mountains had to be purchased through Les' distribution warehouse in California. Growth was explosive. His crews installed many miles of the specialty pipe and thousands of valves; when it became mandated by law as a part of the building code (for most edifices), even more was needed and installed.

"Monty, it was the best investment I ever made," Les confessed to me one afternoon at the race track.

Les made millions in profit from distribution and installation of the modern systems. Some of that money bought him numerous vintage race cars worth a considerable fortune. I was lucky enough to receive a personal tour of his collection of historic race cars; housed in his first building, the old Quonset hut. Twenty vehicles, ten vintage Porsches and ten Fords: GT40s, Cobras and historic racing Porsches, all of them significant and valuable... not bad for a plumber.

What did I learn from Les? Like John, he was the first to admit he was in the right place at the right time. Les had a passion for what he did; he liked being a hands on plumber. Enthusiasm for his work kept him looking for innovation; the next big thing in plumbing. Les found it and aligned himself with the right people. He could have shrugged his shoulders when he heard rumours of a sprinkler system with on/off capability and said, "It'll never catch on." Because he was an expert at what he did Les could recognize an opportunity. More importantly, he acted on it.

Les was also a sole proprietor; the boss. He paid his employees more than the going rate and surrounded himself with smart people. If you said you could perform a certain task by an agreed time, you had better live up to your commitment or Les would soon find someone who could.

Part of the right time and place equation that Les and home-developer John shared was their location in Southern California. Les had plenty of opportunity to tailor sprinkler systems to many buildings and John had ample land on which to construct homes. Both businessmen had countless customers at their fingertips. Les and John are extreme examples of how wealthy a person can become from humble beginnings.

Knowing where to earn a living, make deals and develop a business is very important to succeeding. Large cities will usually provide more opportunity than being located in the middle of nowhere. Even with access to the world (via computers) it is still advantageous to be where the action is. Like it or not, that is usually in an area where people are gathered in great numbers; cities.

The ability to observe economic activity in your chosen city isn't too difficult. Are people moving away in record numbers? Are they building new tracts of housing? Are businesses in the downtown area boarded up and vandalized? Is there a market for what you sell?

Working in harmony with trends is much easier than trying to establish a market where one doesn't exist. This is one of the greatest lessons to be learned from Les' and John's experiences. Which leads to another example of a man (and his market) that I had ample opportunity to observe and learn from.

Fairly-Honest-Bob, as he jokingly referred to himself, operated a small restoration company in Vancouver, Canada. Half a dozen mechanics in his employ repaired/maintained/restored collector cars for local enthusiasts. Bob's small operation specialized in European cars: older Porsches, Ferraris, Aston Martins, Jaguars, Alfa Romeos, etc. Just some of the marques that arrived for minor repair or full-blown, nut and bolt restoration.

Bob's knowledge of just about every European sports car was encyclopedic. Make, model, engine displacement, horsepower, years produced, options available, original tire size, type of fuel injection, length of wheelbase; Bob could cite facts and stats on Euro cars better than a computer. It was his passion.

Bob aligned himself with two friends; fellow enthusiasts that owned numerous collector cars. The three men decided it would be a grand idea to join forces and rent a shop where they could tinker on their cars. Shop space would be big enough to accommodate the three amateur part-timers and maybe a full-time professional mechanic who could perform more involved tasks the trio weren't capable of. The shop evolved from a hobbyist's enclave to a bona fide restoration facility over the course of a few years.

Three industrial garage bays instead of the original one; six employees and a fairly steady workload of customers' cars (along with the three partners' autos) competed for floor space. 'Classic Restorations' was a going concern. Bob surveilled his little empire from the second floor office where hundreds of automotive books surrounded him. His two partners went about their full-time jobs and would drop in from time to time to see what was happening and maybe put a little dirt under fingernails by twisting a wrench on their toys. Both partners had substantial wealth to support their sports car habits. One, a prominent West Vancouver doctor, the other, a successful diamond merchant that operated internationally.

First few years (late 1980s to early '90s) of business at the little restoration company flowed smoothly. Beside coordinating incoming restoration work, Bob would occasionally buy a project-car and have his mechanics do a few repairs and try to turn a profit with its resale. Sometimes it worked, other times it did not. Brokering deals also kept Fairly-Honest-Bob occupied; putting buyer and seller together of exotic cars and collecting a small fee from each was part of what Bob loved to do.

Middle-aged Bob cultivated a network of contacts around the world; always on the phone, talking cars, chain-smoking cigarettes, making things happen. He was good at it. What Bob wasn't particularly talented at was hands on knowledge. Didn't possess the ability to work with tools or machinery. He was a disaster whenever a wrench found its way to his hand, fortunately that didn't happen very often. More than one valuable sports car would need to be re-adjusted after Bob performed his magic. How did I know this? I was one of the mechanics in his employ.

Bob's lack of technical knowledge would sometimes cause the shop to lose more money than it should. His habit of venturing off on his own to examine someone's old sports car would often result in the rusty project arriving at the shop; its previous owner quite happy to have sold it to Bob for top dollar.

"Stitched up again," that's what our most experienced mechanic from Britain would say about the latest Fairly-Honest-Bob project to roll into the shop. Bob wanted a silk purse made from a sow's ear, with a shoestring budget and... he wanted it yesterday. A certain amount of tension existed when Bob tried to insist that, "Anyone can restore a car." He had expert knowledge and experience in certain aspects of the collector car world; restoring/repairing/rebuilding them wasn't that area.

As a young man, fresh out of university (with degrees in commerce), Bob embarked on a thirty-year career as an efficiency expert. Reams of spreadsheets and quarterly reports from a corporation would land on his desk; Bob could pour over numbers and see where the company might realize more profit.

"By trimming the workforce in sector four by 1.8% the resultant savings in labour of 12.8% would translate into a pretax west-coast-division gross return of 3.8 basis points, which, as you know, would increase the dividend on preferred shares by four-fifths of a cent, resulting in a gain of market share by possibly 2%."

Bob issued verbal and written reports of such nature for many years; rarely visiting a factory or seeing an operation in person. Bob told me he hated just about everyday at his job and harboured the fantasy of working with exotic sports cars. That opportunity presented itself when fifty-year old Bob assessed his life after an amicable divorce from wife number two.

"Life is too short to do something you hate," Bob explained to me one day as his reason for leaving a well-paid career of crunching numbers. Convincing two of his wealthier car-loving friends to join him in renting a three thousand square-foot industrial bay to play with their toys wasn't difficult. For a couple of years the boys played well together. They had a full-time mechanic to help with complex tasks and occasional jobs on friends' exotic cars to offset the rent.

Bob's personal funds were dipped into on a regular basis to make up any shortfall, same with the partners. Doctor and diamond merchant did not mind paying to play, they could afford it. Bob decided to make the classic-car garage more efficient at paying its way and convinced his partners that two bays and more mechanics working on customers' cars would pay the bills and a small wage to Bob for his full-time effort at making it happen. Agreed. Two bays quickly morphed into three; before anyone knew it "Classic Restorations" (with six mechanics) needed more effort on the leader's part to break-even each month.

The point of repeating certain facts is to show how a person's previous training and work experience can carry over to a different situation. On paper, the numbers indicated to Bob (from an efficiency point of view) it would be cost effective to expand. In practice, because Bob had minimal hands on experience at repairing/restoring classic cars and wouldn't confer with experienced mechanics as to the effort/hours/material/parts/etc. involved with a job — expansion proved counter productive.

Monthly deficits caused Bob much stress, he'd pass that angst onto his mechanics and try to convince them where they needed to be more efficient. Mechanics would often pass that right back to Bob and include a sentiment such as, "You wouldn't know your ass from an 'efficient' hole in the ground if it jumped up and kicked you!" Quite often said technician would quit, sometimes Bob would invite him to leave.

Patterns of behaviour had been established; with each month's deficit needing to be covered, Bob would put in some of his personal money and hit up his partners for the balance. More work would be brought into the shop by Bob to cover arrears. Up-front payments by new customers would be used to cover past obligations in a Rob-Peter-to-pay-Paul scenario. Bob would medicate his self-induced stress with excess coffee/cigarettes/whiskey and berating inefficient underlings for not producing to his imagined standard.

Sometimes a small profit for a month would be shown to Bob's increasingly nervous partners; usually as a result of bringing in a restoration project that came with a large cheque (of twenty-five thousand or so). The vehicle in question would sit in a corner while its money was used to cover previous obligations on 'Paul's project'.

This format continued for a couple of years, all the while, Bob tried to hit a home run. Brokering a collector car of exceptional value would yield a commission of several hundred thousand dollars. Numerous deals involving exotic automobiles (valued in the millions) were bought and sold by wealthy enthusiasts around the globe. Some of the exchanges were facilitated by Bob's contemporaries in Southern California, Japan or Germany. Fairly-Honest-

Bob wanted in on the action and expended a large amount of time networking with fellow brokers and collectors trying to find a multi-million-dollar deal that would land him a two-hundred grand pay off. The grand slam deal never happened. This was the early 1990s, economic conditions had changed dramatically.

Mid to late 1980s were exuberant days in the field of collector cars, values rose rapidly as more players wanted in on the game. As economic cycles go; prices rise and fall. A ripple of a recession swept around the world in the early 1990s, knocking the value of most exotic vehicles downward. Bob was aware that prices had taken a hit. Monitoring auction results from established sales events around the world gave very clear indication of actual values. Extremely valuable (million-dollar and up) collector cars were recession-proof and maintained their high prices no matter what ups and downs happened in the economy. Lesser vehicles that were in the hundred grand (or under) category were affected dramatically; most prices were cut by half.

Bob was inspired by a brilliant notion; instead of trying to make a large commission on one deal, why not earn many small commissions on a large amount of car sales by staging his own auction. His two partners were persuaded to fund the idea; Doctor, Diamond Man and Fairly-Honest-Bob formed the Classic Auction Team. This would be a large affair, compared to the small-scale history of Vancouver's previous collector car auctions, operations that featured twenty or thirty vehicles on a Saturday afternoon, once or twice a year.

Bob convinced his partners the local market could support an auction weekend featuring a hundred and fifty (medium and higher-priced) automobiles. It couldn't. The first of Fairly-Honest-Bob's Classic Auctions proved to be a well-attended, financial-flop. Less than ten percent of the vehicles were sold. A successful auction will see seventy percent (or more) of the collector cars going to new owners. Bob, not deterred by the large amount of money lost on the first auction was persuaded to have another go at it. His partners decided they had lost enough money, a lesson had been learned; both men terminated all involvement with Bob.

"If you build it, they will come," Bob quoted the old adage as he explained to me his strategy; go it alone. Over the next few months Bob closed the restoration business and rented a small office in the same industrial building where he and a secretary worked full-time at Classic Auctions. To fund the venture, Bob sold his home and placed the money (nine hundred thousand [1990s] dollars) in his bank. Promptly borrowed the same amount of money and placed it with his stockbroker. Bob intended to make his money grow by instructing his broker to place funds where Bob felt high returns would flow: junior-mining stocks.

Over the next few years Fairly-Honest-Bob staged numerous auctions. All were popular, as the rented venues which showcased the well-advertised affairs brought many people to see a high-class auto auction. Actual sales however, proved to be quite low. When the dust settled on each venture, Bob had lost money. He became a little more aggressive with his personal investments to try and compensate for the deficits; riskier stocks that might return bigger prof-its. Didn't happen. Half a dozen auctions and nu-merous investments later found Bob in a bind. He was broke.

As Bob's dream of establishing Vancouver as the next exotic car auction capital of North America wound dramatically down, his health followed suit. Lung cancer... a few months later, Fairly-Honest-Bob passed away. Age: sixty-four.

What did I learn from Bob?

An uphill battle can be very costly; in time, money, pride and health. Attempting to create a local mar-ket can be extremely difficult, especially if trends in the national economy are proceeding in the opposite direction. Digging your heels in and stubbornly throwing money at a lost cause is not dealing from a position of strength. Bob showed that it is possible to align yourself with skilled, experienced, talented, monied people and not put their wisdom to positive use. To be a contrarian is sometimes profitable, most of the time it isn't; particularly if your local market shows signs it is not the right place and time.

Deciding to pursue a passion later in life may come with patterns of behaviour that have been set through decades of practice which can create an inflexible approach to working with others. A rigid way of doing business will often lose money. Bob wouldn't consult with his very experienced mechanical staff in matters of establishing realistic budgets for customers' restoration projects. I saw this numerous times and witnessed alienated customers and frustrated mechanics shake their heads in disbelief at how stubborn the boss could act. Same with listening to the advice of his wealthy partners, Bob would discount their words with a wave of his hand.

Losing money and customers (as well as your reputation) is a sure way to create stress for everyone. Providing a quality product at a fair price is a better way to grow your business.

Finally; self-induced problems can cut your life short. A very experienced, elderly man told me something when I was quite young that has stuck in my mind, "There are only two types of people: those that create problems and those that create solutions."

People who create more problems than solutions usually lose money rather than generate profits. Coupled with being self-employed, more often than not, those people will find themselves dealing from a position of weakness and scrambling to cover losses. Look at the men and women around you, take the best positive aspects from each, learn from that; leave the rest.

Enough about Fairly-Honest-Bob. Time to visit a man from Portland, Oregon.

I became acquainted with Doctor Lou during my time in southern California. Lou and my employer (house-builder John) were friends and sometimes shared driving duties during endurance races when rules stipulated co-drivers were required. Choosing Lou as a co-driver was a good choice. Slightly younger Lou (born in the 1930s) was a very talented man at the controls of a race car.

Doctor Lou was born into comfortable circumstance in Portland, Oregon. As an only child (of prominent physicians) he was raised in an environment of privilege and learning. Young Lou could do as he pleased, but even a well-to-do child has to serve someone; Lou's demanding mother laid down the law in most aspects of her only son's life.

Lou, a physically fit individual in his early fifties, rolled into the parking lot of John's race car shop in Costa Mesa, California, behind the wheel of a Bluebird motor-coach. The type of luxurious conveyance a successful rock band would utilize. Lou's rig was custom-built for him in the early 1980s. Price tag: quarter of a million dollars. Dr. Lou knew exactly what he wanted in a motorhome and had his Bluebird coach tailored to his needs, including enough diesel capacity to drive nonstop from southern California to up-state New York. Every option, from remote-controlled blinds on all internal windows, to a dash-mounted screen to view traffic behind while highway cruising were just a few of the options that were unthinkable in the 1980s. Nowadays they are common place.

Dr. Lou; man of precision, came by his intense character honestly. Like all of us, he was a product of genetics and environment. Brought up in a household where both parents held prominent positions in the field of medicine, there existed certain expectations, "Number one: you will be a doctor." His mother's statement contained no wavering. Both parents imbued young Lou with a certain appreciation for precision, goal-setting, striving for excellence... and along the way... a certain brashness of attitude.

Slight problem; Lou had no desire to be a doctor, hated just about everything involved with the field of medicine. Mom and dad controlled part of young Lou's inheritance and allowance, a proviso existed: grandfather's trust fund could not be accessed without the title of Doctor being earned. As a practical young man, Lou played along; attended one of the best schools his parents' money could secure.

Lou became a doctor and satisfied his trust fund requirements. Followed the simplest path of educational effort... Lou became a dentist. Trust fund money came available to him at age twenty-five, unlocked by the title "DDS". Lou said his mother could barely contain her lack of enthusiasm at him becoming a dentist.

Back in Portland (after his graduation as a medical professional), young Lou tried his hand at dentistry. Hated it with a passion. Was poised to purchase the practice of an elderly dentist. "Monty, I couldn't do it. I knew if I dug into that first open mouth I'd be stuck there for the rest of my life, I would end up another depressed dentist that took his own life. So I walked out. I was a Doctor for a day!"

His decision not to practice medicine in Portland and continue the family legacy didn't sit well with his parents. Threats of losing his inheritance held little sway as trust fund money came available. Lou searched for a business opportunity that would return sufficient profit to allow him to pursue his passion: racing cars.

Didn't take long. Through his family's vast network of associates, Lou found a business that proved to be a diamond in the rough. With an input of effort and leveraged funds, Lou transformed a macadamia nut facility on the Big Island of Hawaii into a profitable venture. With a steady stream of income, Dr. Lou could fuel his need for speed. Minimal amounts of time would be spent at his factory to ensure everyone knew who the boss was and what was expected of them to remain employed. Maximum time dedicated to his passion of racing sports cars (over the next three decades) defined Lou's life.

Doctor Lou was a winner. Whatever racing vehicle he could rent, purchase, co-drive, co-own or coerce to pilot, he did with a certain passion and enthusiasm that blended nicely with his drive to be the best. Lou's reputation as a talented, no-nonsense, man-of-precision served him well in his career. Unlike most drivers, Lou did not need to earn a living and chose to align himself with people, teams and cars that would serve his purpose, rather than being a paid pawn with a professional team. Lou enjoyed a certain amount of control; liked things done with precision. We'll call it 'Lou's way'. From the mid-1960s till the early 1980s, Dr. Lou was in demand as a Hot Shoe. His reputation as a Hothead sometimes limited opportunities, but that did not alter Lou's intense behaviour.

Lou could fly into a rage with very little provocation. The person he aimed at on a regular basis was his long-suffering girlfriend. Gail had been with Lou for many years and was quite accustomed to his very loud, verbal assaults. A chip-clip not placed properly on a bag of nachos after lunch would cause Lou to lose it. Multiple expletives would be barked at his loving partner. "This is how you put the damned clip on the bag so chips stay fresh! How many times do I have to tell you!?" Lou included numerous F-bombs in his tutorial that Gail would endure. She would calmly respond without sarcasm or anger, "I'm sorry Lou. I'll try to do better."

Lou would find something in Gail's performance almost daily that required a verbal barrage. When asked in private about her boyfriend's behaviour, "Lou is actually quite loving and generous, but as you've seen he can be intense. I'm used to it." Gail was unfazed by Lou's tirades.

Dr. Lou had a job for Dennis and me; build a race car. Dennis and I were (home builder) John's full-time employees that maintained his stable of race cars. Big Dennis was my boss, a very capable and experienced race car fabricator that took me under his wing and taught me many things about the world of fast cars.

Lou knew exactly what he wanted. Every detail on his extensive build-sheet of his ideal race car was the product of experience. Lou's precise nature and keen mind had every nuance of his project worked out. Gear ratios for each race track; engine size, torque, horsepower, wheel and tire combinations... just a few of the dozens of particulars on Lou's clipboard. Components to be utilized in the Can-Am series car were numerous; a reflection of Lou's vast knowledge and experience as a successful racer.

Very little was open for discussion. Lou vividly described each component as he painted a verbal picture of his winning race car. How each piece would mesh and work together; his ability to visualize, then translate his ideas was uncanny.

John (our boss) gave approval for Dennis and I to build Dr. Lou his car. A few days later one of Michael Andretti's used Indy-Car chassis rolled into our shop. The engine-less, one year old (spare car) was no longer state-of-the-art for a high-profile team of Mr. Andretti's status. It would serve Lou's purpose in the revamped Can-Am series rather nicely. Dennis and I went to work.

With a watchful Dr. Lou camped in the parking lot (and Gail preparing every meal) we had a race car ready for testing in five weeks. During our whirl-wind build, Lou would occasionally lose his temper with Dennis (not to the extent he would with Gail) and try to make his point in a tantrum. Patient Dennis would merely end the tirade by standing next to Lou and stare down at him. Lou stood barely five and a half feet tall; Dennis: six foot seven. Lou would adopt a quieter tone as Dennis calmly towered over him.

Dentist Lou never yelled at me, probably for a couple of reasons: I was very precise at what I did and I often talked at great length with Lou about his favourite topics... himself and racing.

What did I learn from Dr. Lou?

First: the power of having a precise plan and exact goals. His clipboard had the date of when the car needed to be ready for its first test. Lou had weekly dates outlining the progress of his project.

Second: visualizing every aspect of a major undertaking allowed Lou to write specific goals to monitor advancement of the task.

Third: Lou aligned himself with quality people and worked with them, letting them know his vision and sharing all specifics and goals. Each weekly goal accomplished was cause for the team to celebrate.

Fourth: Lou's intensity of character could easily be controlled by the recipient; Gail, Dennis and myself all had our own techniques of channeling or nullifying Lou's quick temper. Things would have been quite different with two hotheads in the mix.

Fifth: even with his volatile ability to fly off the handle, Lou had the anchor of a specific plan that kept him focused on the big picture; when unexpected small problems arose he dealt with them in a surprisingly calm manner. Usually.

A final word on using visualization to improve performance. A technique serious racers utilize at tracks around the world to try and be better than their opponents. In a sport where the difference between winning and losing is measured in hundredths of a second, any advantage is put into practice.

On more than one occasion I watched Lou walk the length of a race track; established racing venues he had driven countless times. Patiently (and by himself) Dr. Lou would stride towards a corner, close his eyes and see himself at the controls of his latest ride. Brakes, acceleration, steering input, gear selection; every parameter of his performance would be analyzed in his mind's eye to calculate where slight improvement could be eked out. Someone as serious about winning as Lou was, would do the same. On a regular basis the fifty-something dentist would be on the podium celebrating a victory, while better funded and quicker-reflexed twenty-somethings had eaten his dust for an entire race would be looking up to him.

I learned from Lou the power of applying the mind's eye to any project. Setting specific goals (from long-term, i.e.winning a championship, to short-term, i.e. weekly goal on a car build), writing them down and making them public. Most people have no specific goals, only vague notions of doing better; they usually accomplish very little and wonder why at every New Year they make more resolutions that will never be realized.

Dr. Lou had a plan, goals, a budget, the ability to visualize, communication skill and a certain intensity that kept people on their toes. His ability as a leader (by working with the team, rewarding accomplishments, focused intensity and winning) commanded a certain level of respect. Most of the time he tried to raise his voice in a berating fashion was based on an actual lapse in performance by the recipient. Only rarely did he go over-the-top in a super douche mode. Lessons were learned from Lou.

Alan and Amelia: a married couple from Vancouver serve as our next example. Bit of an anomaly; she was the dominant economic factor, while he brought a spin to their story that caused them to be a more powerful team.

I knew Alan and Amelia as individuals before they became newlyweds. Both in their forties, their union was Amelia's third marriage and Alan's first... or was it?

Alan and Amelia shared a love of fine automobiles. She, being born in Britain, loved Aston Martins. He (Canadian?) was fond of Italian sports cars, especially Ferrari. Not able to afford something with Enzo's name on it, Alan did the next best thing and drove a Fiat Dino.

Amelia could afford to indulge her automotive desires. Raised in an affluent household, Amelia then married into a noble family. She departed that first union with a healthy monetary settlement and no children. Not being terribly disappointed with the return on that investment, Amelia did it again. Second husband was rumoured to have paid more than the first.

Inheritance came next; speculation of particulars was fodder for numerous British tabloids. Amelia took it in stride, her regal posture and erect bearing were a reflection of an upper class education. She spoke with an accent the Queen of England would approve of; carrying herself with a certain grace and decorum, Amelia exuded confidence that bordered on brashness. I liked her.

Skinny and slightly stooped, Alan sported a full head of thick, black hair and a hearty moustache that provided needed contrast to his pale skin. A quiet talker, not given to outbursts of laughter, Alan was a contrast to Amelia's more overt character. As a research scientist employed by a world-class university department, Alan could talk at length about life from a molecular level. I liked him.

When I heard these individuals from very different worlds had wed, my initial reaction was, "What an odd couple." Meeting them as husband and wife proved to be an insight into human chemistry. The equation balanced; something in the whole brought each to a new level. It wasn't gushing honeymoon antics, no; merely a calm position of equity. I liked them.

Then the rumours started, "Did you hear about Alan?" "Is that his real name?" "What have you heard about Amelia?" "Is she dying?" "Will they go to jail?"

A local newspaper contained a couple of paragraphs calling Alan a Person of Interest. Reportage stated Alan being questioned by authorities regarding his activities as a university student while attending a New York City Institute in the 1970s. Interesting.

For the sake of brevity (as the details of what transpired in Alan and Amelia's lives over the few years since that first paragraph appeared could fill a book), I shall limit my recounting of their story as it was told to me by Alan and Amelia in person.

Dust had settled; Alan could look back on his story and tell the facts, Amelia added colour-commentary as we sat in my shop on a sunny Saturday. Lessons from their tale can be learned and put to profitable use in any circumstance. Back to the story.

Alan wasn't Alan, nor was he Canadian. His life on the west coast of British Columbia was a marked contrast to his past. Born in New York City to upwardly mobile, middle-class Jewish parents, Alan was known to his family and friends by his given name... Christopher.

Chris and his brother (David) came of age in the 1960s, a turbulent era; New York City was an epicentre of social unrest and protest. As a student at the Rochester Institute of Technology, twenty year old Chris/Alan helped organize and participate in some of the student causes. Marches and sit-ins devoted to eradication of war or legalizing marijuana were par for the course. Chris and company were, "Making a stand, taking it to the man."

Chris, the agitator/student activist, was approached by an undercover cop (posing as a fellow student) and willingly sold him twenty dollars worth of mind-expanding LSD. Promptly arrested, tried and sentenced; young Chris was bused upstate to serve a four year sentence. His prison was the maximum-security institute famous for harsh conditions: Attica. 1971 was not a great year in the prison's history of human rights. Chris was welcomed to his new home by an ice-cold, fire-hose shower. Pressure of the blast pummelled his skinny, naked body against a concrete wall, leaving numerous bruises and a hint of what was in store.

Over-crowded Attica was no place for a lightweight, cerebral student with long hair; a petty drug dealer. After a few months of Attica's madhouse antics his jailers agreed and transferred the quiet student further upstate to a minimum-security facility. Outdoor work was the norm at his new home. A great deal of freedom compared to Attica. Still, being an advocate for social reform, quiet Chris organized his fellow inmates to protest for better conditions. Didn't take long for authorities at the minimum-security facility to single out Chris as a troublemaker.

A bus ride was scheduled to return student-activist Chris back to Attica (August 1971). News of the latest conditions at the maximum-security prison reached the inmates up north at the same time. Chris did not want to return to the harsh prison; nor could he keep quiet about treatment of his fellow convicts.

Something had to be done. Chris came up with a plan of action befitting his radical mindset: escape.

Turns out it was quite easy; Chris merely walked into the woods from his work detail. Hiked through the forest a few miles and found himself in Canada. Connected with sympathetic draft dodgers that helped him establish a new identity and hitchhiked to the west coast of Canada. Chris was now... Alan.

For three decades Alan lived a quiet life in Vancouver, British Columbia, Canada. Established himself with a good job as a research scientist, became skilled at blue-grass banjo and cultivated a keen interest in vintage cars... never once returning to the United States. Family in New York City and a few, trusted individuals were the only people aware of his new life.

News of his father's death reached fifty-year-old Alan/Chris via his younger brother David. Alan felt it might be safe to journey to New York and attend the funeral. After all, he was a married man and carried a Canadian passport. Feeling bad about missing his mother's funeral many years previous also influenced Alan's decision.

Amelia knew the details of her husband's life. Alan was equally aware of Amelia's history, including her breast cancer treatment that had kept the illness controlled for numerous years. They married one another despite their stories. Time for an adventure; travel to the United States.

Breaching the border was a breeze for the middle-aged couple; no alarm bells. Attending the funeral and reuniting with relatives (and brother David) was a bittersweet affair. Once dad was in the ground, talk turned to the will. The small estate was to be shared by the two brothers. A difference of opinion arose. David argued he had no brother; any brother he once had turned his back on the family, and furthermore, was a fugitive living in Canada under false pretences. Valid points.

David stood his ground; he wanted all. Alan made a stand; birthright is the deciding factor, no matter what happens in a person's life, a son is entitled to his inheritance.

The discussion continued through heated, long-distance telephone calls over a few weeks. Alan and Amelia didn't give a second thought to how easy it was to cross back into Canada. That is, until a knock at their door by an officer of the law. David had blown the whistle on his older brother. Time to answer a few questions.

David figured with his brother engaged in a legal mess he could do what he wished with the inheritance. A bureaucratic battle was on. Alan placed a legal hold on the contested will, while he and Amelia faced an onslaught of inquiries from offended entities.

State of New York, Immigration Canada, United States customs agents, Passports Canada, Canadian Border Services, judicial systems in two countries; the list seemed to grow on a daily basis. Media sources received wind of the story and the quiet couple found themselves in the spotlight while things unraveled... in public view.

Alan and Amelia's dirty-laundry-story played out for two years as legal volleys shot across the international border. Many angles, by all entities, made for interesting articles in newspapers from Vancouver to New York. Alan's age; length of time from crime; petty nature of original infraction; Amelia's battle with cancer; standing in the community; length of original sentence, there was no limit to the amount of stories that could be spun from Alan and Amelia's predicament.

Weariness of the two year battle had caused Alan to reach a decision; he would surrender to authorities and take his punishment. It was a gamble. Could be behind bars for two years, or more; might be out in six months, nobody could give at exact answer.

A relatively quick victory at the onset of his saga saw Alan settle with his brother. Birthright ruled: the two brothers shared proceeds from the sale of assets. Funds were limited, Alan had spent most of his inheritance in the exhaustive legal battle. Amelia and her husband had an agreement; all costs were to be paid by Alan, it was his mess and Alan accepted financial responsibility. Part of the reason to surrender to authorities was based on Alan's dwindling Deal Bag.

Back at Attica, cut off from any communication with the outside world, prisoner Alan received a welcome from his jailers. A powerful fire-hose blast of cold water had his naked body pressed against the same concrete wall of thirty years previous. It was 2001, exactly three decades had passed since his last shower. Guards had a good laugh. Not much had changed. Still, an older, wiser Alan put his head down and took his lumps; determined to do his time.

Alan and Amelia's story generated a fair amount of interest on both sides of the Canada/US border. A double-edged sword of attention put authorities under a spotlight; they did not wish to be viewed as weak... nor overbearing. Balance must be achieved; four months of incarceration was deemed the right amount. A relieved Alan sprang from Attica a free man. Just had to square himself with Canadian authorities... small matter of assuming the identity of a deceased infant thirty years before.

Slap on the wrist from Canada and all was right in Alan's world. The newlyweds awoke from a thirty month nightmare with a clean slate. They had been through an ordeal that would have torn most couples apart. Yet, their refiner's fire forged a stronger bond between them.

What did I learn from Alan and Amelia?

Number one: importance of full, honest disclosure between partners. Imagine how different their lives would have been had Alan not told Amelia he was once named Chris. They were stronger and more united because of their shared burdens.

Number two: they had monetary parameters of what they would (and would not) do. Alan and Amelia were in their predicament as a couple; Amelia could have used a small fraction of her wealth to drag out the legal battle for many years, but she didn't. They had an agreement; his mess, his money. Simple.

Same lesson can be applied to deal bag money, it has one purpose: to make money. That clarity of vision was exemplified by Alan and Amelia, even though they couldn't predict an exact end date to their predicament, they had precise rules of engagement, loyalty to one another, plus full and honest disclosure... all three factors helped them grow stronger as a couple. Valuable principles we can learn from.

Finally: know when to throw in the towel. Legal battles can be very expensive, last for many years and be stressful. Having seen numerous people involved with protracted divorce proceedings and/or court battles, most of the participants involved usually comment that if they were to do it again they would have been better off walking away from the mess in the early stages. Even Alan admitted he would have surrendered to authorities a lot sooner were he to have a 'do over'.

Thinking about Alan and Amelia's situation will give ample opportunity to draw parallels between your struggle to overcome obstacles... or... what appear to be insurmountable problems in the moment. Sometimes we become overwhelmed by the immediacy of what is surrounding us on a daily basis. That is when you need to step back, take a breath, and tell yourself in a calm voice, "This too shall pass."

Peter McGale... this person represents someone I have worked with and observed for many years, in fact, a life-time... my father. To set aside the familial connection and look at a parent from an unbiased point of view can be difficult. Especially when said person may have administered a spanking or two; one (or more) might have been deserved.

Mr. McGale was certainly a hard worker. At thirty-five years of age he (and his long-suffering wife) had seven hungry children to feed, shelter and clothe. For most of his working life Peter was a self-employed, small-businessman. From being the owner of a laundry and dry cleaning enterprise (employing half a dozen people) to a one-man shop that built wheel balancers forty-years later.

Between stints at being self-employed, and spread over a career that spanned six decades, Pete would earn a paycheque in a field he had a certain talent for; sales. Usually employed at large, new-car dealerships, where his ability at persuading people to part with large sums of money would garner him a decent income. If an audit of Peter's income over many decades were to be conducted, it would be obvious that his greatest compensation (per hour of work) came from being employed by others and simply taking home a paycheque. As we have seen, being your own boss can be very profitable, especially if you are in the right place at the right time. Conversely, being the owner of your own business can be very challenging, time consuming and a money-losing-proposition. Most small businesses fail to return enough profit in the first few years to stay open, reasons for such a high amount of failure are as numerous as the people involved. We'll focus on Peter's experience and what we can learn from his career.

Pete's ability to earn an income from the variety of businesses he owned and operated had its ups and downs. As every self-employed person knows, long hours of effort can go unrewarded and it seems there is nothing but frustration as payment, whereas other times, money flows as though one has struck the motherlode. Peter experienced both ends of the profit/loss spectrum for many years and knew there were never any guarantees of steady income while being a small business owner.

Certain talents are required of a person that wants to be his or her own business operator. Peter had the smarts to realize it's always advantageous to align yourself with people that are better at certain skills than yourself. My father enjoyed the sale's process; meeting people, figuring out their needs and making sure they were happy with the deal. Lacking in his personality (at times) was the ability to command respect; Pete sometimes had difficulty insuring customers paid their bills. To that end he usually hired a person that could firmly (but politely) see to it that the few people who took advantage of his generous nature paid their bills in a timely manner.

The realization that you can't be all things to all people was part of Peter's business philosophy that guided him in hiring employees that had abilities in areas he didn't; paperwork, accounting and bill collecting. At least, that is the way Pete was for most of his career, his last decade as a one-man show brought a dramatic change. A change in his basic character and how he viewed the world.

A lengthy process of life's wins and losses chipped away at Pete till eventually a toll was taken in his seventh decade. For most of his life everyone admired Pete's quick wit, good humour, generosity, positive attitude and ability to persevere when others would have quit. Most of those traits that made Peter a very likeable man had vanished by the time he turned seventy. I'm sure he didn't intend to become a grouchy codger, but he did.

Having to work in order to augment the small government pension that he and his wife received was a difficult process. Pete's final venture saw him manufacturing a wheel-balancing system that required a moderate amount of physical ability that his health found increasingly difficult to deal with. A decades-long struggle with digestive disorders became more severe and served to limit his mobility. Peter started to become noticeably cranky and irritable. To someone who hadn't seen Pete in many years the shock of his diminished physique and edgy personality was a negative surprise. Instead of being the warm and inviting person that everyone felt comfortable around, Pete would often launch into a paranoid monologue about 'them' and 'they' preventing his latest invention or product from total marketability.

Peter had hoped his last business would be a grand slam home run, when it didn't grow in the leaps and bounds the way he had dreamed (and told everyone it would), a great amount of enthusiasm was replaced with a growing bitterness. The transformation happened in his early seventies and coincided with a general deterioration of his health.

My father's life and details of his career, both as an employee and boss of his own businesses could fill many chapters. To reduce his history to a few pages is merely to illustrate a few points of character that we can learn from, and not to show disrespect, as any of the businessmen I have had the good fortune to work with could serve as subject matter for many volumes. Peter's life needs to be reduced to a few lessons in keeping with this book's format. To that end; what did I learn for my father? And what can the Blue-Collar Riches student apply in his or her life after looking briefly at Peter's experience?

First: some people are meant to be self-employed. Second: it is beneficial to say, "I don't know."

Third: there are two types of inventors: open and closed.

Fourth: it is more profitable to be respected than trying to be liked by everyone.

First lesson. Being self-employed is not for every person. Those that are meant to employ others (and people who have a desire to be independent) usually know who they are; developing a business is often a natural evolution of that desire. For example, a young man that loves working on cars soon finds that his evenings and weekends repairing friends' vehicles returns more money (and fewer hassles) than his full-time job at a car dealership. Before he knows it, he has rented a small garage and is in business. Forty years later he may have five employees and a profitable repair shop; his debt-free building is then sold to augment his retirement.

Conversely, there are people who are better suited to work a regular shift as an employee. That person can also earn a great deal of profit in their spare time pursuing a passion. I know a number of fellow gearheads with regular jobs that purchase decent used cars and sell them into different markets at great profit. One imports a couple of vehicles each year from Japan and regularly makes a good profit from his specialized knowledge of right-hand drive, Japanese sports cars.

My father was meant to be self-employed. He had the ability throughout most of his career to say, "I don't know." This served him well, as it allowed him to hire people that were qualified to say, "I know how to do that."

We are all familiar with a know-it-all; the person who boastfully claims to be capable of any task and stubbornly attempts to complete what is asked of him, too proud to ask for help, he will boldly charge into a task and sometimes succeeds, despite his lack of knowledge and experience. That is perfectly fine on your own time, however, when someone is paying you to do something they aren't capable of doing, you had better be qualified to do the job.

Toward the end of his life, Peter lost the ability to say, "I don't know" and became more rigid of attitude, to the point of being bitter and paranoid. That second lesson of being able to admit you don't know something will ensure you stay flexible of mind, willing to learn from others, and be humble. A more open attitude almost always returns greater profit.

Third point. Open and closed inventors. Having worked with a number of creative men (that brought numerous products to market), it is necessary to say a few words about Buck; a man very similar to my father who I had the good fortune to work with.

Buck was an 'open' inventor. He wasn't always that way. In his early years Buck was very closed about the inventions he wanted to market. Paying for patents, trademarks and ensuring that anyone who worked with him signed nondisclosure documents was all part of Buck's early career... a very expensive way of doing business. Buck learned being 'closed' was a money-losing way to conduct affairs.

"A patent only gives you one thing: the right to defend yourself," Buck told me. "You're better off just building and selling whatever you've invented, if someone feels you are infringing on their patent, then modify it or move on to the next idea."

Buck had learned through many years of experience how the game was played. In his industry of trucks/trailers/transportation/road-building/etc., many improvements came and went. He had observed it was more advantageous to talk with people and figure out a better way of doing things by bouncing ideas back and forth; an open approach to invention that created a greater flow of ideas and solutions. Then he would produce his product. "Without making patent lawyers rich," as Buck would say. "And if somebody slaps you with a Cease-and-Desist-Order after it's been on the market for five or six years, then you know it's time to move on."

Buck told it like it was, an old-school fabricator/inventor that built stuff and had the flexibility of mind to change tactics/production/course or direction almost instantly. In most cases the open approach to idea sharing and invention is the path to a rich life.

My father became increasingly 'closed' about inventions and ideas as he neared the end of his career. Attempting the lone wolf approach to developing products and marketable ideas is to limit yourself to possibilities that other minds can bring to the

129

process. Sharing thoughts opens an endless forum of possibilities. Living in fear that someone might steal your idea will keep you 'closed' and limit every-thing... except your paranoia.

Fourth idea. It is more profitable to be respected than trying to be liked by everyone. We all possess personality traits that can be beneficial in terms of realizing the goal of building wealth. Determining what flaws in your character detract from profitable deal making is a step in the right direction. Are you too nice? Do you want every person you deal with to like you? If my father had one flaw (that cost him many dollars from numerous deals) it was the way he often wanted people to like him; usually by being too generous.

A small group of people would regularly take advan-tage of Peter's generosity, either through missed payments on vehicles or directly asking for cash. Sob stories of every type would come into Peter's office when he was a car dealer; more often than not the storyteller would leave with a hundred dollar bill in his pocket and/or a tank of gasoline in the truck he bought two months back.

Being known as a soft touch (in sticking to the principles of a deal) isn't operating from a position of strength. If people know you can never say no when solicited by a dubious cry of help, that small group of people will beat a path to your door and 'like' you forever. If this is part of your personality and it is your desire to command respect, rather than succumb to being a victim of peoples' approval, all you have to do is... practice. Practice what you're going to say ahead of time, plus; have specific goals for your money, equipment and energy.

"No, I can't lend you my truck for the weekend."

"Nope, can't help you move, I have another commitment."

"Sorry, my money is invested in another sector."

"Not this year, we have already set our charitable budget."

"You have missed three payments, the sheriff is empowered to seize the truck."

"If you need a loan the 'Cash Store' can arrange an advance."

Just a few phrases that can be on the tip of your tongue; ready to be stated with quiet purpose, not disdain or anger.

Only you can adjust the practiced responses to your situation. I can assure you it works. Before you know it, the practiced replies will become habitual. In a business environment where numerous people come through the door every day, there are many people with their hands out each month. This may not be applicable to your situation, but if it is, you are better served by commanding respect with a straight-faced reply to a person that attempts to solicit something from you they don't deserve.

Instead of becoming angry at yourself (after the fact) for handing out another fifty bucks to a person that took advantage of your weakness, you have the ability to change.

More profit will be realized pursuing a path that commands respect. Having a clear set of rules on how you conduct business is a simple way to weed out the few people that will try to take advantage of you. Sticking to your rules in buying and selling will establish a reputation of fairness.

Time to examine another person's experience at earning respect...

Russ, a minimum wage, blue-collar worker in his late twenties that transformed his situation and embarked on a path of building wealth.

Russ and I (along with three others) were roommates; we shared living accommodations in a run-down, old house in Vancouver, British Columbia, Canada. I became familiar with Russ and his story; watched him progress from employee to self-employed.

Back in high school, Russ' best friend was Rocco. Together, the two fifteen-year-olds would earn a bit of spending money by helping Rocco's father on occasional Saturdays. Hard work, building muscle as labourers with his dad's masonry crew. Moving brick and stone, digging holes, mixing cement and general grunt work had young Rocco and Russ feeling like exhausted 'rental mules' at the end of a day's work. Old-school, Italian stone-workers were Russ and Rocco's examples, hardened men with calloused hands and strong backs.

After (barely) graduating from high school, Russ became a full-time labourer alongside his best friend Rocco, joining the small crew of seasoned masons. The older Italian men schooled Rocco and Russ in many skills: smoking, swearing, drinking, brick laying, stone-splitting, trench digging, mortar mixing, muscle building, hard work and loud laughing.

Being low man on the totem pole meant Russ performed more of the grunt work. Rocco; being the boss' son gave him elevated status and a much higher wage. This was the norm for many years.

For a decade Russ quietly went to work, learning and observing. Splitting rock, building retaining walls and beautiful stone stairways that blended with the landscape. How to construct with block and brick; mixing mortar and cement according to weather conditions were just a few of the many skills honed by muscular Russ. Working outdoors year-round, gathering experience and expertise while earning minimum wage. No job security, no benefits, no paid vacations; just plenty of callouses and exhausted muscles.

Rocco became the boss when his father retired; business as usual, Russ (still low man of the group) did most of the dirty work. Occasionally, Russ would be left alone on a site as the half-dozen other masons tended to other jobs. Russ was skilled in all aspects of his trade, including giving potential customers estimates.

Russ had accompanied Rocco on numerous occasions to peruse the yards of many West Vancouver homes with their owners. Being familiar with the cost of materials and what to charge for a hand-made, split-stone staircase or retaining wall was part of the job. Russ could do it all, yet he was paid only a tiny bit more than minimum wage... even after ten years of working with his friend.

During his decade of informal apprenticeship Russ would occasionally find himself without work for several weeks each year as the senior men were put to work first. Even though he received a tiny wage for the amount of work he performed, Russ decided it would be wise to save a hundred or more dollars each month to tide him over when there was less work. With great pride, Russ announced to his assembled roommates that, for the first time in his life, he had ten thousand dollars in the bank from his years of saving.

Russ had no specific financial goals, just the notion of having some money on hand for the times when work was scarce. Then he hit on the idea of buying a house. That's when he came to me with the notion, we looked at the feasibility of what Russ was thinking.

Price of a small house at the time (mid 1990s), in and around greater Vancouver, was a quarter of a million dollars. Russ had ten thousand dollars, a job that paid slightly more than minimum wage, no credit history and had nowhere near enough money to make a decent down payment. His expectation of purchasing a house was unrealistic.

Russ and I discussed his situation over a period of weeks; an hour or two here and there, kicking ideas back and forth. At first glance, Russ appeared to be a little slow, yet took the time to consider most proposals and the amount of effort involved. He persisted with the idea of owning a home; I took time to point out the carrying costs that landlords rarely mention: maintenance, insurance, equipment, repairs, security, interest, renovations, taxes, etc.

As we examined Russ' life and his future, one thing became evident: Russ was an expert at what he did. More than a decade working with old-world craftsmen had given twenty-something Russ a wealth of experience and knowledge. Specific questions I asked yielded exact answers; from prices of services, to types of rock and the characteristics each possessed. His knowledge of stone and masonry was astounding. Time to plant a seed.

"How come you're not self-employed?"

"I don't know."

"You've been left alone on numerous jobs to do most of work, haven't you?"

"Yeah, sometimes."

"How much do you get paid?"

"Bit more than minimum wage."

"Can you build a retaining wall by yourself?

"Hell yeah."

"Do you know where to buy all the rock, cement and supplies?"

"Yes, been doing it for years."

"What would a decent one-ton dump truck cost?"

"A good one might be thirty thousand."

"Do you know how to find the people who want stonework done?"

"Sure do."

"Would you be interested in earning ten thousand dollars in a month instead of fifteen hundred?"

"Of course!"

Seed started to grow.

Russ went to work with a different attitude for the next few weeks. Looked at things in a different light; he could do everything his older workmates did. Russ had the ability to write an invoice, make an estimate, network with suppliers and find out who wanted a stonewall or beautiful split-stone staircase grafted into the landscape of their new house.

Behind-the-scenes Russ enthusiastically went to work aligning with key people; dad was on board with the idea of his only son being self-employed and agreed to co-sign for a loan when it came time to purchase a proper dump truck. Russ' sister (an accountant) agreed to assist with registering his future company and how to stay legal with the tax-man.

Russ laid the groundwork of making a transition; he 'could' be his own boss. Certain amount of nervousness tinged his comments as we talked about his possible big step into being his own boss. His greatest trepidation came from loyalty to Rocco. How was he going to tell his best friend that he was seriously considering leaving. How would Rocco react? How would Rocco's father take the news?

"Do you want to work the rest of your life for a small wage as Rocco's slave?" I asked Russ.

"No, not really."

"You need to talk with Rocco. He's your friend. You've known each other since childhood. He'll understand."

"I guess so."

Russ cautiously spoke to Rocco the next day. What Russ feared the most turned out to be completely unfounded. Rocco and Russ had a good laugh. The joke? Rocco and his father wondered how long they could work Russ like a rented mule. How many years could they keep paying Russ barely above minimum wage before the hard working young man came to his senses? They weren't going to rock that boat... more laughter.

Rocco gave Russ his full support, encouragement and more, he agreed to help Russ find work when he was ready.

Russ was floating on air, we talked details.

"I need to find a good truck," Russ said.

"Don't forget business cards and invoices, and a business account."

"Yeah, yeah, I'll get my sister onto all that."

"Start phoning around and visit some car dealers. Spread the word about what type of vehicle you're looking for," I advised.

"If I can find a possible vehicle, would you come look at it with me? You know, inspect it. Make sure I'm not getting ripped off."

"Be glad to," I assured Russ.

Russ spoke to numerous salesman at dealerships and sifted through classified ads looking for a suitable work truck. Didn't take long; couple weeks later Russ was behind the wheel of his own truck. Twenty-five thousand dollars worth of diesel-powered, one ton, hydraulic dump truck; perfect for hauling piles of stone and supplies to a job site. Seventeen thousand dollars of financing (co-signed by his father) left Russ with a few thousand dollars of savings in the bank to buy supplies. All he needed was his first job as owner of Rockstar Stoneworks.

True to his word, Rocco gave Russ his first leads, a couple of phone numbers. Rockstar Russ was driving towards his first potential customer, excited about the prospect of being his own boss and earning a fair return for his labour. Russ approached his first quote with sound advice: Provide quality work at a fair price and receive regular payment.

Russ and I had formulated a business plan. He started from day one with specific steps on how to insure he received regular payment for his work and how to pre-qualify customers as being worthy of doing business with. A couple of rules for potential customers would make sure everyone would be happy. Russ would ask potential clients if they were comfortable receiving an exact quote instead of an estimate. If they were comfortable with that notion he'd continue. Step two: collecting a percentage of the money in advance for material. Russ had clear instructions that if any potential client objected to this rule he was to excuse himself and seek a new customer. This phase would usually happen during the first phone call before Russ even visited a work site. Next: a customer must inspect Russ' work at the end of each week and pay for what has been done, any amendments or adjustments must be agreed upon at that time and written down on the quote.

Rockstar Stoneworks only had a couple of rules for conducting business, a simple approach to keep everyone satisfied.

Russ and his first customer shook hands and exchanged paperwork; a quote to build a retaining wall and a split-stone staircase to match. Price? Ten thousand dollars. Russ collected a cheque (one-fifth the total) for supplies and the agreement to be paid two thousand dollars at the end of each week's work. Russ knew from experience he had four weeks of work ahead of him. That first customer hired Russ for a number of reasons: Russ gave an exact quote (not an estimate) and showed the man examples of his work in the same West Vancouver neighbour-hood.

For the next month Russ worked hard. At the end of each week he proudly showed his customer what had been accomplished and collected another cheque of two thousand dollars. More money than Russ earned in a month working for Rocco. After his truck payment (and a thousand dollars for material) was subtracted from the ten thousand earned in his first month, Russ was paid a fair amount of money for his skill. Rockstar Russ was very happy with his new status of being his own boss.

Securing the next job while working on the first was easier than Russ imagined, before he knew it word-of-mouth had helped procure more work than he could handle. In a few years his photo album over-flowed with images of quality jobs he did for satis-fied customers. Russ was never short of employ-ment. A one-man operation, Russ had no intention of hiring anyone else or expanding into a bigger business. Russ had observed how Rocco's crew worked when the boss wasn't present and realized he wanted to be proud of the finished product and didn't have the personality to babysit employees.

Dealing with wealthy customers and developers was part of the job that kept Russ on his toes. Most of his potential customers were influential people building large homes on the hilly terrain of West Vancouver. Taking advantage of a contractor by various means seemed to be how some of the builders operated; promises of payment or having to pursue settlement for the bill by legal avenues was something Russ couldn't afford to do.

By using his rules of engagement when sizing up a job and a customer, Russ avoided being a victim of an unscrupulous developer/homebuilder and collected his weekly payment for work accomplished. Russ avoided the bad seeds and didn't have to threaten to leave a job half done in order to coerce payment for his quality stonework. Dealing from a position of strength insured Russ received prompt and full payment, most of the time.

About five years into Rockstar Stonework's career, Russ and I had lunch; caught up on old times, had a few laughs. Russ had come a long way in a short time, was a home owner; after three years of saving large amounts of money, he put a substantial down payment on a suitable house in North Vancouver with plenty of room to park his work truck. Two roommates payed rent (which covered the monthly mortgage nicely) and there was always plenty of masonry work. For the majority of his work Russ received payment as agreed; thanks to his pre-qualifying of clients.

"I've only been ripped off once," Russ said as he pushed his plate aside after lunch.

"What happened?"

"Did a job for one of Rocco's good friends."

"Let me guess, Rocco vouched for him."

"Yup."

"Just a handshake deal? No paperwork? Said he would pay you at the end of the job? In cash?"

"Yup, I even gave him a discount, should've cost him ten grand, only charged him eight. Built a beautiful stone oven in his backyard with a curved retaining wall behind it. 'Bout a month's hard work."

"Did he pay you anything?"

"Not a cent."

"How long ago did you do the work?"

"Two years back."

"Learn any lessons?"

"Yup."

Russ gave a shrug of his shoulders, it wasn't the money; more of an opportunity not to drop his guard and always stick to the successful formula of doing business, realizing he wouldn't be in business very long if he didn't have a specific way of qualifying customers and collecting money for his work. Learning an expensive lesson by his one lapse of following his plan confirmed to Russ how important it is to stick to his specific way of dealing from a position of strength.

Being self-employed was the best thing that could have happened to Russ. I'm glad I played a small part in assisting twenty-something Russ to take the plunge and become his own boss. As of this writing (2015) forty-something Russ is in a financial position of strength. House is paid off; plenty of money in the bank. New truck; lots of work to keep him as busy as he wants. Bachelor Russ still has roommates paying him rent. Vacations each winter in sunny locales make Russ happy he decided to become his own boss many years ago.

In his twenties, Russ arrived at the conclusion where his skill, compensation and confidence were out of sync with being a minimally paid employee. The fact Russ needed a bit of a nudge and some advice from someone who could look at his situation from the outside serves as a reminder that seeking guidance from people you respect is always wise. Like most successful people, Russ invested in himself.

Russ is very representative of what can be accomplished from humble beginnings. Even though Russ could never be accused of being overly book smart he possessed a character trait far more important in order to succeed... perseverance.

At any point in his informal ten-year apprenticeship of becoming a skilled mason he could have quit and pursued any other low paying job. He didn't, he hung in there and worked liked a rented mule because he loved his work. Enjoyed building with brick, block and stone. Sure, he could have made the transition to self-employment many years sooner, that's beside the point, we all have 20/20 vision when looking at the past.

We can learn valuable lessons from Russ's example in how to transform minimum wage into maximum wealth. Russ isn't a millionaire but he is in a comfortable position of financial strength, able to weather any downturn in the economy and be the master of his own destiny. Are there parallels in your situation compared to Russ?

The Hungarians. Time required to save a Deal Bag of twenty-four or twenty-five thousand dollars can be cut in half when two people of similar goals work together. For a moment, think of the possibilities when a determined group of four people combine their efforts. Time for two stories: one of a united front (Hungarians), the other of a young married couple at odds with their finances and how both teams dealt with saving money, their Deal Bags and investing.

As a married man in my late twenties I managed a thirty-six unit, three-story apartment building. My wife and I occupied one of the units. Managing the building required a couple of hours work each day, in exchange we received our accommodations rent-free. An excellent job, I enjoyed every day of work. With most rental buildings in a large city (in this case, North Vancouver, British Columbia) there is a certain turnover of tenants. Part of my duty was to screen potential renters and decide who should be allowed to live in the building. Having done the process numerous times, I became fairly comfortable in the role of determining who would be a reliable rent payer and how to spot deadbeats.

Three bachelor (studio) apartments in the building meant one of them rarely came up for rent. They were small; basically a single room that was kitchen/living/dining room and bedroom all rolled into one. A tiny bathroom completed the suite. Typically, a single person would rent a 'bachelor'.

One bright spring day I was pulling a couple of weeds from a flower bed near the front entrance just after I put out the 'for rent' sign, which had Bachelor slid into the slot indicating what was available. Five minutes into my gardening, a group of four people were at the front door. I saw they rang my buzzer. They indicated an interest in renting the small apartment. When informed that a bachelor suite was suitable for one person, they politely asked if they could tell me their story and what their goals were. They had my attention.

The two married couples were in their mid-twenties and told me it had taken a few years to complete the paper-work and process to move to Canada. They were from Hungary and told me their goal was to live as inexpensively as possible for however long it took to save money to buy a house. They also intended to open a business when their English was better. In the meantime, they intended to work at whatever job they could find in order to start saving money.

By this time I had sized the foursome up as a very focused and earnest team. I knew I could depend on them to pay the rent. Only one catch: the bachelor was intended for a single person, not four... if the landlord received word four people were occupying the suite, we would both be in trouble. I took a chance with them. The little apartment had been vacated the night before by a tenant with very little furniture who did a 'midnight run' and forfeited his damage deposit. An hour later the quiet Hungarian couples moved in; one suitcase each and a caseload of determination.

Over a year and a half I watched them accomplish their goals. They lived out of their suitcases with only the meagre furniture left from the previous tenant; not even a television. The men found work as labourers with a construction crew that payed just a bit more than minimum wage. Early each morning the wives would prepare a hearty lunch for the boys and they would wait on the corner for the bus ride to work. A few hours later the gals would be picked up by their employer that took them to their work as cleaning ladies. Minimum wage.

With their rapidly amassing monies (four incomes, no kids) they splurged and bought two mattresses; cheap ones. A few months later the quartet were the proud owners of a used Camaro. It served them well to explore the metropolitan area of greater Vancouver. By this time I was fairly friendly with the dependable youngsters and delighted in hearing of their progress.

About a year into their adventure they had saved enough money to lease a waterfront bakery, just two blocks down the hill from where we lived, at the prestigious Lonsdale Quay (pronounced "key") shopping centre. They were now confident with their English (and knowledge of Canadian tastes) to open a pastry/cake/sweets shop. A trade they were familiar with, being accomplished pastry chefs in their native country of Hungary.

All four now worked at Laszlo's Pastry, two blocks from home. Business was good. They catered to the tourist trade... and those that appreciated (and could pay for) quality.

Six months after opening their store it was time for the next goal; home ownership. They gave notice and happily announced they had purchased a large duplex in a nice neighbourhood a half mile away. When asked if they were going to occupy both halves of the duplex, they were true to their character. They had a goal: rent half and all four would live in the other half until it was paid off (in two years!). Then they intended to occupy both halves and start families as the next milestone in their lives.

Occasionally I would chat with the happy quartet at their pastry shop and receive an update on their progress.

English they spoke was excellent. Two cars were parked in the garage of their duplex, home was paid off, business was booming and one of the wives was expecting the first child. Smart people with realistic goals that went from strength to strength because of their unified approach.

The four Hungarians represented a winning team with everyone aligned and committed to the same goals. By living frugally, staying focused, persevering and sacrificing immediate comforts with an eye toward long-term financial strength, they succeeded in realizing what they set out to do.

Now the other story: What happened with me during the same period? I was married to a beautiful, headstrong, Italian woman. We had immigrated to the west coast of Canada, much like the young Hungarian couples. That is where the comparison ends. I, being Canadian, knew how Canada functioned and tried to prepare my Italian wife and mother-in-law for their new way of living in a different country and culture.

Arriving in Vancouver, the three of us moved into an apartment in the building I would later become the manager of. My wife and I were childless (by choice), in our late twenties and ready to begin a new life in Canada. We had a plan, or so I thought.

Before landing in Canada, my wife (Stefania) and I had many occasions to discuss how we would earn a living in the New World. Our intention was to purchase a fixer-upper house in a good neighbourhood, live in it, make repairs, add value to it; then sell it for a profit. To do this we both intended to find jobs and work on our project house on weekends and spare evenings. Mother-in-law ('Pina) was also onboard and would keep herself busy in a support role by preparing wonderful meals and taking care of domestic duties. We were a team with the plan.

My life savings in the summer of 1988 was seventeen thousand dollars. Not much in the grand scheme of things, but enough for a start. A modest house (in need of some work) in a decent neighbourhood of North Vancouver could be purchased, at the time, for around a hundred and twenty thousand dollars.

The plan was to rent an apartment, secure employment; then search for a project house suitable for our skills, budget and time frame. June 1988, we landed in Vancouver, Canada. Within a couple of days we rented a two bedroom apartment in North Vancouver and I found employment three blocks away at a large Ford dealership. My income secured, it was enough to feed us and pay the rent. Time for the next phase: find a project house.

Even 'Pina (mother-in-law) agreed with the plan, as she and her (deceased) husband did something similar in the postwar, rebuilding years in Italy of the 1950s. They had a small blueprint business and invested their money in apartments. 'Pina and her husband profited from inside knowledge of where projects were to be built and made a comfortable nest egg for themselves. 'Pina (widowed) agreed with the plan.

Within a couple weeks of landing in Vancouver, I found a diamond in the rough. On a double corner lot, one block east of the prestigious Grand Boulevard area of North Vancouver, sat a lovely little house of about nine-hundred square feet. A realtor's sign on the front lawn. Without calling for an appointment I took a chance and knocked on the front door. Very friendly man (in his early eighties) greeted me. We talked about his life and the house. I was treated to the whole story as we wandered through his little home.

Just after the Second World War (in the late 1940s) he and his expectant wife managed to scrape together enough money to purchase a double lot in the recently surveyed area of North Vancouver. Old-growth trees covered the hillside. Trees cleared to create streets were hewn into lumber at the local mill. A few brave souls that bought lots in the area purchased said lumber and started to build. My elderly friend and his brother constructed each others' houses while working full-time jobs. With help from many friends and neighbours, they shaped their community, creating solid, comfortable, but humble homes.

The little house was a gem, not much to look at but it was surrounded by bigger, modern homes that replaced the old timers. His children were grown and gone, wife had recently passed away; he realized he didn't have the strength to maintain the house.

Asking price of a hundred and twenty thousand (1988) dollars was fair. I made arrangements with the realtor to view the house with my wife and mother-in-law. Great excitement filled me at the prospect of this first deal.

The plan of adding value to the solid house was explained to Stefi and 'Pina as we viewed its interior. We would live upstairs and over the course of a year, I would finish the basement. This would require a bit of sacrifice as there would be times of noise, dust, busy weekends and not much money for extras. Pay off a year later would be quite substantial. The idea of selling the house and repeating the process on a larger scale was accepted as reasonable. Both ladies were excited and contributed enthusiastic suggestions about their involvement.

After discussing the deal with 'Pina and Stefi, I put in an offer two days later of a hundred and ten thousand dollars. It was accepted. I was prepared to put ten grand as a down payment, leaving me seven thousand in my Deal Bag for closing costs, taxes and miscellaneous charges. We had a plan.

Monthly payment on a mortgage of a hundred thousand was about seven hundred dollars, just a few dollars more than the rent of our two bedroom apartment; easily affordable. We contemplated the transition of moving out of the two bedroom apartment and into the fixer upper. Stefi and I went over all the ins and outs. Including the fact there would be a life insurance policy on the mortgage; in the event of my death, the mortgage is paid out and she would receive ownership of the property, free and clear. Stefi understood. We had a plan.

A few days later we went to the bank to sign mortgage contracts. Friendly lady at the bank guided us to her office and we noticed her name was Italian. She and my wife exchanged small talk in their native tongue. All systems were running smooth. Folder of official documents was opened and the first of many papers was presented and explained. I signed the mortgage contract and slid it towards my wife. Her mood immediately changed from jovial to confrontational. Anybody familiar with women of Latin birth knows how quick this can happen. Flick of a switch.

Poor bank lady didn't know what hit her, nor did I when Stefi loudly announced she had no intention of signing any documents. Claimed she didn't know what was happening and there was no way her or her mother's money or possessions would be used to benefit me, her husband. The verbal assault flew fast and furious, completely out of left field, in English and Italian. Banker and I were wide eyed and stunned. Embarrassed? Unbelievably so, felt like choking the life out of my wife, if only to shut her up. Patient bank lady tried to wedge a word in edgewise while Stefi continued her verbal tirade. Banker quietly tried to explain the facts of the matter... in Italian.

Stefi had a hard time listening as she continued her non-stop assault of words. Banker tried to bring my wife to a tranquil place using logic, reason and factual statements.

"Only your husband is responsible for the monthly payment."

"You and your mother will not have any assets used as collateral to secure the mortgage."

"If your husband dies, you receive the property free and clear."

"Your husband can't receive a first mortgage in British Columbia without your signature."

Did not matter how the berated-bank-lady or I talked with Stefania, she would sign no paper. Half hour later we were out of the bank. No mortgage. Me? Speechless, livid, ready to kill. We had a plan.

It was the beginning of the end of our marriage.

A day later, the kind lady from the bank called. We talked. In her many years of arranging mortgages, she had never experienced anything as dramatic in her office. She felt so bad, my 'nonrefundable' down payment of ten thousand dollars was returned, nor did she charge me for preparing the documents. Nice lady.

What of the house in question? Later that month it sold. A small developer bought the little house and wasted no time in tearing it down. A large, attractive duplex replaced the old home. It fit into the neighbourhood nicely and didn't look at all like a typical duplex. Ten years later it came on the market. Asking price? Three quarters of a million (1998) dollars. Sold immediately. Glad someone did well.

Let us compare our two tales. The Hungarians' success in dealing from a position of strength and my situation; not what could be called advantageous.

Trying to save money (or invest it) can be difficult or fairly easy. It can be done alone or with like-minded people. Saving money or putting it to work in any investment will be practically impossible if you have a significant other who isn't onboard. A very simple concept; one I learned the hard way.

Rule number three of Blue-Collar Riches is about saving as much money as possible while living a frugal lifestyle. In two years a single, determined person should be able to bank close to twenty-five thousand. Imagine what the four Hungarians accomplished with their unified front. Even a minimum wage can return dramatic results when like-minded people focus their combined efforts.

Should you find yourself aligned with someone who doesn't share your goals (of sacrifice to build financial independence) you need to do everyone a favour and end the relationship.

For many years I read numerous books about buying and selling real estate. Talked to many people who were actively involved in flipping properties. I had developed a passion and looked forward to my first deal. Experience in house construction and renovation was part of my past, applying that expertise to making a profit in real estate wasn't in the cards as my wife didn't want to be on the same team. As my marriage crumbled, it was time to rely on my other area of enthusiasm to start making profitable deals; collector cars.

Seventeen thousand dollars in my Deal Bag wasn't a grand sum of money. At the time (late 1980s) I didn't refer to my money as a Deal Bag, merely as savings that had eroded from twenty-four thousand of the previous year. Proceeds from the sale of a sports car I owned. Marriage had chipped away at my account quicker than my income could replenish it. Time to change that.

With no need of my wife's signature, I transformed that seventeen thousand into fifty-five thousand dollars in the span of a few years. One collector car deal at a time. Not a huge amount of money by most standards. More important was the implementation of goals and techniques of buying low and selling high. Ten rules of Blue-Collar Riches started to gel, then received a further spurt of growth when I devoted every dime of the fifty-five thousand to a two-year project that yielded true wealth. That's another story, subject of later chapters (and an entire book).

'Deals' section of this book will assist in honing 'buying low and selling high' skills. First, however, you must consider the art and practice of the ...

Chapter Four

Lowball

We are all familiar with the phrase: Buy low, sell high. The tried and true formula to make profit. Most people focus too much effort on the 'sell' part of a transaction. Asking too much money for your collector car (or whatever you are selling) is not dealing from a position of strength. There exists another saying: Everything sells if priced right. You are better served (and will make more profit) by concentrating on the 'buy' side of a transaction. That is where the art of the lowball needs to be applied.

As soon as you say lowball most people have a negative reaction. Associating the term with unscrupulous dealers of used cars (thanks in part to movie images that continue the stereotype), is the usual thought that comes to mind. However, if I were to say, "Far more profit can be realized in the 'buy' side of a transaction by utilizing one simple strategy..." you would be very interested to learn more.

Specific techniques of offering a lowball number will be given. First, it is beneficial to understand some of the reasons why a person would even entertain the notion of listening to you and your offer in the first place. Most of the reasons a person wants to sell something hold true; whether they are trying to part with an automobile, a piece of antique furniture or a painting hanging on the wall. One simple reason may be they have grown tired of looking at it.

A 'project car' sitting on the driveway in front of a house, collecting dust and rust, waiting to be restored to its former glory can be an eyesore. Let's just say it might be an issue between husband and wife. Someone might be motivated to clear the driveway, at any price. My experience with this type of seller is fairly consistent; he'll put on a brave face and say something like, "I don't really want to sell it but..." and launch into a story about his life going in a different direction. It is your task to open him up by 'general talk' and then try to unearth the real reason for the sale of the beloved item. Reading between the lines of comments will help determine the level of desperation. Exasperation on the part of a wife (or significant other) is a common reason for items being sold.

Carrying cost is another. Example: a good friend of mine bought an E-type Jaguar, all in pieces, completely disassembled. Purchased it from a man in his eighties that had stored all the parts for thirty years. Not only did he pay monthly storage, the old man also moved everything from Vancouver to Toronto... and back again in the three decades. Paying to move and store an old car for many years isn't cheap. Even though the Jaguar was a desirable 'Series 1' from the early 1960s, I doubt very much if he came close to covering his storage expense with the sale of his project.

Logic overcame the aged man's stubbornness and he realized he no longer possessed the enthusiasm, skill or money to complete his retirement project. My friend, who purchased the pieces, had the ability (and shop facilities) to restore the Jaguar. He bought it for a song and went to work. Looked like a new car after a year of full-time effort.

Which leads to another reason why some vintage vehicles are for sale (and can be purchased well below their actual value); death. Had the elderly Jaguar owner of the previous example passed away before he had a chance to find a good home for his beloved 'basket case' chances are he would have died and left the mess for his wife to deal with. More often than not a grieving wife will clear out a pile of automotive parts for pennies on the dollar.

Should the widow have an 'advisor' with her to assist in the settling of her husband's affairs, be prepared; this person may, or may not, have any expertise. Best thing you can do with an 'expert' is ask very specific questions.

"How many E-type Jaguars have you restored?"

Chances are he has no depth to his façade and you have taken a great step in nullifying his influence on price. In the rare case that the friend/advisor is the supreme expert in the field of Jaguar restoration (and has a firm position on the asking price) you would be wise to walk away. There is always another opportunity to profit on the 'buy side' of a deal just around the corner. Deal from a position of strength.

Estate sales can be great opportunities to purchase collector cars. If the format is an auction, you simply need to do the math and know well ahead of time how high to bid before things progress to a fast-paced auction where emotion can overtake your logic... and before you know it you end up paying too much. Again; deal from a position of strength.

Another motivating factor behind a person's decision to part with a vintage vehicle at a bargain basement price: divorce. Similar to death, marital problems can offer a potential low-baller many opportunities to find the next money making project. Assets need to be divided and sold. Cash needs to flow into lawyers' coffers. An angry wife may find herself in possession of a 'damned' car that her ex loved more than she felt he should have and will part with it for the first offer that arrives.

A woman scorned can be your invitation to enter into the next money making venture. At this point I need to relate the story of a half-million dollar Italian sports car and its 'near death' experience. I have first-hand knowledge of the very rare Osca in question. Its handmade aluminum body needed my services as a metal restorer; this is how I came to know the facts of the matter.

An Osca is any Italian race/sports car built by the Maserati brothers. The particular model in question dated from 1952. One of six to exist. Rare? Yes. Valuable? Certainly. Should it have been hauled to a dump and disposed of? Only a person of dubious mental status would contemplate such a thing. This is precisely what happened. Well, to half of the car. Here is what transpired...

After a lengthy career of racing, the little four cylinder Osca was purchased by a wealthy businessman in Southern California; mid 1970s. Parked in his two-car garage at home, the hobbyist wasted no time in starting his restoration. Every part he could remove from the lightweight sports car was set-aside and the stripped chassis sat on four jackstands. Like many projects, it languished in this state for a number of years.

Lady of the house did not take kindly to her parking spot in the garage being occupied by scattered parts and an old race car. It became a source of many heated discussions. While on a month long business trip to Japan, the husband was unaware of his wife's level of scorn. She hired a junk hauler to cart the entire project to the dump. His first load included the engine, transmission, front and rear suspension, radiator, wiring harness, gas tank, gauges, seats, wheels, headlights, steering wheel, taillights — everything that had been unbolted from the chassis.

Fortunately, a curious neighbour saw what was happening and intervened when the junkman returned. He asked a few questions and was shocked when told the exotic Osca parts were now at the dump. With a few dollars from the neighbour (into the junk man's hand), the two of them removed the chassis to the safety of his garage next door, out of the clutches of the absent businessman's wife. For all she knew, it was at the landfill where she believed it belonged.

Neighbour then rushed to the dump to recover what he could. Too late. Bulldozer had moved a mountain of debris onto the precious bits. Lost forever. One can only imagine the reaction when the proud Osca owner returned from Japan.

Divorce proceedings commenced almost immediately. Stripped Osca chassis was purchased for a pittance by its present owner who embarked on a thirty-year, worldwide search for parts. That is where I entered the scene, to commence restoration of the aluminum body.

Learning the story behind his project serves as a reminder that crazy people tend to do crazy things, someone has to be there to pick up the pieces. Could be you.

Along the way to divorce, many people will deal with their stress in different ways and provide more reasons for selling something at rock-bottom prices. This can take the form of destructive behaviour: alcoholism, drug addiction, infidelity, gambling, extreme sports... or any number of activities that serve as a distraction from the marital situation. You can be there to purchase what is being sold. Don't feel bad about offering a lowball price, remember... they created the problem, you are there to offer a solution, however brief, to their circumstance. If you don't buy their car/painting/comic book collection/ antique desk/motorbike (or whatever) at a deep discount, then someone else will. The less you pay for their goods; the more profit you'll make. Simple.

Another motivating factor why a person may offer something of value for a very attractive price: illness. Many types of sickness affect our nation, one area that encompasses a large amount of people but receives very little attention is mental-health.

I am not an expert in the specialized realm of mental health, however, having been involved in a relationship with a girlfriend that was hospitalized numerous times in our seven years together, I used the opportunity to learn about maladies of the mind. Primary source of information was a prominent psychiatrist that treated my girlfriend and her manic depression (Bipolar syndrome). According to him; one in five people suffer from some form of mental disturbance. Given the population of North America, that is an astounding amount. Manic depression, schizophrenia, obsessive-compulsive disorder and depression are just a few of the ailments that can affect a person's brain and their actions.

According to the doctor; more hospital beds are used for mental illness than anything else. Cancer and heart disease take a backseat to the amount of resources dedicated to mental disorders.

Nevertheless, people (on or off) their medication will sometimes do what seem to be strange things. They may sell their hot rod for pennies on the dollar and board an airplane to Las Vegas, then gamble the proceeds, losing it all in a matter of minutes. Another person will be convinced the sight of the dark blue, 1966 Maserati in their garage is the source of suicidal depression.

Two examples that were real; I knew of both men and their collector cars. Found out about each deal after the fact. Point is; mentally ill people, like anyone else, will sometimes do things that defy explanation. Such as; sell a car dirt cheap, someone will be there with money in hand, might as well be you.

Numerous reasons exist that pressure a person to sell something at a deep discount, procrastination is one. New job in a different city that forces a move; collector car can't possibly make the journey, stubborn owner holds on till the last minute, hoping (by some miracle) that his beloved muscle car (and all the boxes of parts) could somehow fit in the moving van and find a hidden spot in the small apartment across the country. Not going to happen. It's the eleventh hour, desperation sets in. You arrive on the scene with cash; as a potential purchaser (dealing from a position of strength) you have leverage. If the seller baulks at your low offer you can walk away, knowing there are many other opportunities in the city.

"Wait, we might be able to make a deal." Words that could come from a person's mouth that has stubbornly put off parting with their pet project till the last minute. Let the seller make large moves in price while you make tiny ones. Strength.

Conclusion. A person will be motivated to sell something for various reasons. Uncovering the level of desperation and degree of emotion is your job. General questions, listening and taking time to read between the lines, are important in the initial phase of determining whether you can proceed to a lowball offer. Remember your goal going into each transaction. Mine was: A hundred percent profit on each car deal. Yours may be slightly different. Just knowing your objective will help structure how you give a lowball offer.

Has the seller indicated a level of motivation to sell? Yes? Good. My general rule: offer roughly one third of their asking price as a starting point. Not a hard and fast rule, each situation is slightly different. Don't act arrogant. Offer a statement like, "I am prepared to purchase your '67 Mustang today, with cash, the value it represents to me as it sits is forty-two hundred dollars." Then close your mouth and let him respond. Do not utter another word while the offer is being mulled over, let him know you're serious by your quiet, confident tone. If you have done your home-work, he'll respond with a counter offer closer to your number than to his asking price.

In all my experience of buying I've never encountered a person that was offended by a starting-point-lowball-one-third-asking-price-offer. Where-as, most potential buyers I speak to are afraid to present such a low initial amount. These are the same people in other conversations that scoff at the notion of my goal of making a hundred percent profit on every collector car deal.

The counter offer your seller comes back with indicates how ready he is to part with his car, doesn't matter what he states along with it. He may say something like, "Forty-two hundred is too low. I rebuilt the transmission three years ago: new clutch, pressure-plate and throw-out bearing. I have a stack of receipts I can show you. How about eight grand?"

He's asking you a question, with a certain amount of hope and resignation in his voice. Do not respond in the same manner by asking a question, instead; make a confident statement. "I can go to forty-four hundred." Again, shut up so he has a chance to see you are serious. Do not say a thing. Do not justify your number with any other words. Do not wander away. Do not look at the car. Do not fold your arms. Do not roll your eyes. Do not kick a tire. Quietly and confidently stand there, looking him in the eyes.

Wait for his reply. You are there to solve his problem. This is very important. He is dealing from a position of weakness. You can walk away and find another opportunity.

You will settle on a price much closer to your number; every time. Deal from a position of strength. In the unlikely situation that you don't come to an agreement, give him your name and number and leave. Stating you may or may not be interested if he should call.

Many books have been written on the art, science, skill and specific techniques of negotiating. Subtleties of the buying and selling process fill volumes in every library. I can only encourage you to continue learning, as knowledge and experience combine to create wisdom. Wise is the person who can profit from their positive application of expertise, goal setting and perseverance.

Chapter Five

Deals

Numerous examples of my Deal Bag transactions with collector cars will be found in this section, most of them, positive and profitable. I'll start with an account of the sale of an Alfa Romeo sports car. Time and effort involved with the transaction put it in the 'negative ledger' and hopefully its recounting will illustrate the need to keep accurate records of names, dates and important details.

Losing money on a car deal rarely happened. In fact, to be precise, I never lost money on the 1973 Alfa Romeo in question, just time.

A young couple from East Vancouver came to view the GT 2000, 2+2, Alfa Romeo Coupe I had advertised in the local classifieds. Asking price of five thousand dollars represented excellent value for the handsome sports car. She; an artist. He; a musician. They dressed and looked the part; hippie couple, both in their mid twenties. Their search for a suitable vehicle was a major task and it had to be a reflection of their artistic temperament. This was to be the first car they would own as a couple. They needed an automobile with a certain look.

Distinct lines of Italian design that emanated from the silver Alfa Romeo satisfied their sense of aesthetics. They gushed enthusiastically about its handsome European flair. In great detail I showed them the car. Being a (sixteen year old) used vehicle, meant certain items were worn. Took time in the underground parking to show them what was good, what was fair and what was in need of attention. More importantly, if any repair was needed before it could be safely driven: none was so pressing that the Alfa couldn't be operated.

I gave them a grand tour. Drove them around the neighbourhood and onto the highway for a few miles. Back on a quiet side street I parked and we looked closely at the Italian sports car in the full light of day. They loved it. Both drove around the neighbourhood and were excited about how the Italian automobile would complement their style.

Back at my apartment's underground parking, I had them lay on the concrete and I pointed their gaze at the underside of the car. With a flashlight illuminating the suspension, I indicated a broken coil-spring above the rear axle. A component that would need to be replaced at some point but didn't seem to affect the car's ability to be driven.

Two relative beginners to the world of used automobiles.

After a few hours of quality time spent with the young couple I felt I had the right to ask them if they would like to buy the car. I wasn't surprised when they said (practically in unison) they would love to buy the Alfa Romeo.

Next day they arrived with cash in hand. I wrote a bill of sale. Province of British Columbia, Canada, has an official transfer form/bill of sale. Particulars of buyer and seller, vehicle details and sale price are entered. Sale price is sometimes left blank so the purchaser can write whatever amount they want as a seven percent sales tax is charged when registering the vehicle. Doesn't matter if the same automobile is bought or sold fifty times in British Columbia; sales tax is collected each time. To soften this expense, sometimes the buyer will write a lower amount than what they paid.

Hippy couple asked about the possibility and we agreed to write down three thousand as the amount instead of the five grand they paid me.

With paperwork in hand they went to the neighbourhood insurance agent/registrar and returned with a transit-permit. Happy hippies took possession of their Alfa Romeo and drove away to enjoy many miles of motoring. Or did they?

In the car business there is one rule: Buyer beware.

Three weeks after the sale of the silver Alfa Romeo I received a phone call. Unhappy hippies were on the line. They were no longer in love with the car.

First day they had it, they dropped the car at a local garage to have it inspected. According to the irate voice on my telephone it was a death trap, unsafe to be driven. Allegedly, thousands of dollars would be needed to make it roadworthy. Subsequently the Alfa Romeo was parked in their yard. Artistic temperament had stewed for weeks, now they were boiling mad and demanded a full refund.

Patiently, I explained how automobile transactions worked, "There are no refunds, especially with private deals of used vehicles." Both took turns yelling into the telephone, calling into question my character and moral standing.

"How could you be so callous? Selling us a deathtrap!"

They threatened to take me to court. I calmly replied that no judge would side with them, this was a private sale of a sixteen-year-old vehicle (1973 Alfa in 1989). I guaranteed they would lose, and it would also cost them court fees and everyones' time. They hollered some more and hung up.

Two weeks later there was a knock at my apartment door. I was greeted by an attractive lady with a lovely smile.

"Hello, are you Monty McGale?"

"Yes."

From behind her back she produced a legal-sized manila envelope and handed it to me.

"You have been served." Her smile disappeared. She turned and briskly walked down the hall to the exit; I stood there, perplexed.

Document inside was a summons to appear in Small Claims Court, North Vancouver, British Columbia, Canada, April 12, 1990.

"April? That's seven months from now!" I said for my own benefit.

Plaintiffs where the young hippie couple, attempting a legal avenue to receive a refund of the Alfa Romeo's purchase price. Seven months to wait for their day in court. Cost them a hundred dollars to secure a spot in the busy legal system.

Being well informed about the legality of selling a used car as a private citizen, I knew I would win the case. Even though I had never been to small claims court for a car sale, I knew I was dealing from a position of strength.

Months of waiting, day in court finally arrived. Justice would be served. I saw the couple in the court's hall and went to greet them with a hand-shake. A man stood quickly between us and told me not to greet them. They were 'lawyered up'.

We were invited into a mediation room by an arbitrator. Her job was to try and advise us to settle any issue without using the judge's time. Loser of the case would have to pay court costs of three hundred and fifty dollars. Her advice to the unhappy hippies? Drop the case. They insisted the judge would find in their favour and I would be liable for the rcimbursement of their money, plus interest for their 'suffering' and the court costs. Arbitrator couldn't deny them their right to be heard. Her final plea of dropping the issue fell on deaf ears.

Our group entered the courtroom and quietly waited in general seating while other cases were presented. Mostly contested speeding tickets. If the issuing officer wasn't present to tell his side of the infraction, the judge would quickly say to the complainant, "I've heard your testimony, see the cashier on the way out and pay half the fine."

One person, after hearing this started to say, "But your honour, I have"... judge cut him off and said, "I heard your testimony. Pay the cashier the full amount. Next case!"

We were called by the bailiff and seated at two tables in front of the judge. Plaintiffs were asked to tell their story. The young 'lawyer' began to speak. Judge interrupted, "Excuse me. Who are you?"

"I'm a student of the Law and I'm here to defend my clients."

"This is small claims court, no legal counsel is called for, nor necessary. I will hear directly from the plaintiffs."

The 'lawyer' sat down. Hippies (and dressed as such) began their tale. How their lives had been turned upside down since the trauma of the Alfa Romeo purchase. How, on the first day of driving the car home, they took it to a local repair shop and had it inspected. They related to the judge how their mechanic informed them the vehicle was "a ticking time bomb" and "a deathtrap."

Judge interjected, "You drove the car to the garage?"

"Yes. We were shocked by the inspection results, then we drove it home and parked it. Two weeks later we phoned Mr. McGale and wanted to know why he would sell us a deathtrap. We asked for our money back."

"Did you receive a written statement from the mechanic on the unsafe components?"

Hippies, "No, he just told us what was wrong and we drove it home."

"You drove it home?"

"Yes."

You could feel the disbelief in the judge's voice. I knew this was a case that couldn't be won by the young couple. I could have sold them a used vehicle with major parts falling off it and still won the case.

Buyer beware. It was their responsibility to check the car's condition before purchasing. I knew this, so did the arbitrator and judge. Their 'lawyer' should have known it too. Still, stupid people tend to do stupid things.

"I have heard the plaintiffs' statement. Mr. McGale, you have been sworn in, tell me your side of the transaction."

I informed the judge that when the couple initially called they expressed an interest in finding a small European sports car that would suit their lifestyle and not look like every other vehicle on the road.

"They were invited to come and inspect the Alfa Romeo. They arrived and were quite impressed with the car's look. They informed me as to their artistic talents and how important to them a vehicle's 'look' should be.

Judge to plaintiffs, "Is this true?"

"Yes."

Judge, "Continue, Mr. McGale."

"I spent about twenty minutes with them explaining the mechanical systems of the Alfa. I went on at great length how the Alfa Romeo driving experience is different from North American automobiles. They said they loved the look of the interior as I told them of the mechanical nuances of operating an Alfa sports car. When asked if they were interested in going on a test drive they said 'yes'."

Judge, "Is this true?"

Artistic duo, "Yes."

"Please continue."

"I took them for a good ride through the neighbourhood until the Alfa was warmed up, then drove on the freeway for ten minutes. We returned to a quiet neighbourhood where I parked. The three of us admired the look of the car as it sat by the curb. They took turns driving to see how the car felt. When we returned to my underground parking I went to the effort of having them lay on the concrete while we examined the underside with a flashlight. I pointed out a broken coil-spring in the rear suspension and stated at some point in the future it would be a good idea to replace it, but in the meantime, as they had just seen, it could be driven quite safely."

Judged to plaintiffs, "Is this true?"

Plaintiffs (with a little hesitation), "Yes."

Judge to me, "Continue."

"When we stood up I asked the pair If they would like to buy my car. They said yes."

Judge to plaintiffs, "Is this true?"

"Yes."

Judge, "I've heard enough. I find in favour of the defendant. Case dismissed. Plaintiffs will see the cashier and pay full court costs. Next case."

Over as quick as that, less than ten minutes. Hippies were on the verge of tears as their lawyer sat with his mouth open. They rushed out of the room and down the hall towards the cashier. I tried to have a word with them; they wanted nothing to do with me.

Funny thing about the whole affair, even two weeks after the initial sale, I would have gladly refunded their money had they been polite. If they offered to return the car with a full tank of gasoline, or even an apology for taking my time, I would've been happy to find a new buyer; one better suited to the unique needs of an Alfa Romeo. It's been said, "You can capture more flies with honey than you can with vinegar." They turned to vinegar and it cost them.

Part of the point of recounting this tale (in detail) was to describe the proceedings of small claims court. I found it educational to be part of the process. You wait for months, and the time you spend in front of a judge is minutes. You better be prepared if you ever find yourself in a similar situation. My opponents were not. They operated from a position of weakness and it cost them. Being ill advised and emotional in the face of legal-logic (with merely your own sense of justice as a guide) is to be at the mercy of the judicial system. Their 'lawyer' was in the same league as their mechanic; hippies aligned themselves with unqualified people instead of heeding the advice of real experts, like the arbitrator.

I considered the Alfa deal a loser, even though I made a hundred percent profit on the sale, time and aggravation of dealing with silly people is the same as losing money.

Most important lesson learned was the need to qualify my potential purchaser before they laid their money down. I might have been fairly expert at collector cars, but I had a lot more to learn about people. Each deal is an opportunity to gain knowledge.

From an Alfa Romeo to the next opportunity to profit and learn... a Jaguar.

Besides having a goal of earning a hundred percent profit on each collector car transaction, my other self-imposed rule was: one project at a time. The temptation to purchase a second vehicle and have it sitting in the wings, waiting its turn, was strong. I resisted. Fundamental reason? It is best to dedicate all your time and energy to one project without any distractions. Just having another vehicle taking up space (both on the ground and in the one's thought process) robs you of the ability to dedicate all effort to the primary vehicle. I knew I didn't have the ability to serve two masters at once. The realistic goal of only having one project on the go kept me from running around; kept me focused. Experience taught me there is always another deal to be had, no need to stack them up.

Back to the Jaguar affair. With the Alfa gone it was time to find another deal. Pre-Internet days (early 1990s) meant scouring newspapers' classified ads, trade publications (Auto Trader), parts stores' bulletin boards and speaking with anyone remotely connected with the car business were some of the means of sourcing my next project.

Small, one line classified ad in the back of the local North Shore News simply read... "1969 Jaguar E-type, 2+2, $18,500." A West Vancouver phone number included. Initial phase of searching involved making phone calls. Even though the Jaguar was priced at full retail for such a used vehicle, I decided to give the seller a call. Takes very little effort, and you never know what will happen until you try.

A few rings of the phone and I had the Jaguar owner in conversation. My objective was to open him up, start him talking about cars in general, specifically: British ones. A lot can be deciphered about a person's relationship with their vehicle by coming at the topic from afar. Big picture attitude versus asking them something pointed like, "How many miles does it have on the odometer?" Broad questions that require a person's opinion will give you ample opportunity to read between the lines. This will indicate if the person is in love with his automobile or he's angling for a divorce.

Jaguar Man had very few complimentary things to say about the British car industry. Gave me generous clues he was ready to break up with his once loved Jaguar. Decided to pay him a visit; immediately.

The beige, 2+2, Jaguar E-type, with its red leather interior appeared to be in excellent shape. Even in the poorly lit underground parking I could see it was a decent car. Its elderly owner and I talked shop as I carefully inspected every corner of the British sports car with my flashlight. With the hood (bonnet in Brit-speak) open and the straight-six engine exposed, we continued our discourse.

Using general, open-ended questions, I employed a sales technique to coerce him to tell the truth about his Jaguar.

While poking about the engine bay with a flashlight, I asked, "What do you think of the Lucas electric systems that are on most older cars from Britain?"

Noticeably agitated about the topic, Mister Jaguar responded, "You mean Prince of Darkness? Lucas electric systems have to be the biggest problem the Brits ever exported!"

Even though his statement was more opinion than fact, I decided to narrow his focus now that I had him in a mood.

"Has the Prince of Darkness visited your Jaguar?"

"Damn right he has. Don't know how many times I've had a dead battery or been towed to a repair shop."

This is what I wanted, specifics. Bring out emotions and true comments will follow. Electric problems I could handle. I was giving the older man free rein to become angry at his Jaguar. With each passing moment, I knew the value of his vehicle was diminishing in his mind.

"Can we start it?"

"I'd like to, but the battery is dead. Damned charging system."

I had him in confession mode. Told me of numerous occasions that included expense and embarrassment of being stranded with a dead battery. The car was a millstone around his neck. Could I relieve him of this burden?

I let him talk until he was fully vented of his emotions. All the while, I continued my flashlight-inspection. Car was clean. Interior like new, no rust anywhere. I didn't need to hear it run. My gut told me it would be as he claimed, "When it runs, every-thing works the way it's supposed to, usually."

My resolve was clear. Time to see if I could purchase it at my price. With the goal of a hundred percent profit in mind (and maybe an outlay of five-hundred dollars in a worst-case scenario to replace the bat-tery, alternator and regulator) I knew my top dollar was nine grand. He was asking eighteen and a half thousand (early 1990s) dollars; fair price for a run-ning, 1969, 2+2, E-type in great condition. I decided to try an offer. When a lull in his critique presented itself, I spoke... slowly and deliberately.

"I am a little disappointed I can't hear the car run, or take it for a test drive, but, if the price is right, I'm prepared to buy your car, right now, in cash; to me, the right price is sixty-nine hundred."

Before I could blink an eye he said, "Sold." Stuck out his hand to seal the deal and we shook on it. Next fifteen minutes were used to fill in the official trans-fer form/bill of sale and counting out sixty-nine hundred dollars. Relief on the man's face lightened his step.

I removed the battery from the old car and told my West-Van-Man I'd be back in a few hours to drive my Jag away. He smiled. With keys, paperwork and a lighter wallet, I drove homeward in my Pinto station wagon, elated with my latest project.

At home in my little workshop, I wasted no time in topping the battery with water and placing my charger on it. A leisurely lunch with my wife while I told her of the latest purchase.

"I'm kicking myself, should've offered even less than sixty-nine hundred. He jumped on my lowball offer so quick I could have said two-grand and he would've gone for it."

"Maybe something is wrong with it? You said you didn't drive it. Probably has a blown engine."

My wife had planted a tiny seed of doubt. Was the deal too good to be true? Gut feeling of earlier started to fade. Ate my lunch with a side-plate of nerves. Had I bought a dud? Had I been taken by an elaborate ruse? Had I been too greedy? Judgment clouded?

Three hours later my wife and I drove towards West Vancouver. Trusty Pinto station wagon hauled booster cables, container of gas, a few tools and my lovely assistant. I had paid just under seven thousand dollars for a gamble. My gut hadn't steered me wrong in the past... still, this could be a first.

Juiced up battery positioned under the large bonnet of my Jaguar; wife and West-Van-Man chatted amiably as I pulled the choke and twisted the ignition key. I let a sigh of relief as the engine turned over as it should and fired to life. It warmed on high idle as I looked things over before latching the big hood. All systems go. Except for the charging system. Volt and amp gauges weren't doing their usual dance. Didn't matter; had enough battery power to drive home.

Wife and I said our goodbyes to the happy man; waved farewell with a broad smile on his face. Jaguar was smooth as silk, ran flawlessly to my underground work-space of the apartment building I managed. Time to go to work.

Placed probes of my multimeter on the back of the alternator to confirm my suspicion; not charging.

Fifteen minutes later the alternator sat on my workbench. With the long retaining bolts removed, I opened the alternator like a cracked egg. Poked and prodded with the probes of my meter, not really knowing what I was looking for.

A removable diode that seemed like a fuse came out with an easy tug of two fingers. Tested for continuity; had no flow... not a good thing. Could it be the problem?

Bundled all the bits into my reliable Pinto and drove six blocks to Auto Marine Electric, specialty shop that catered to the boating/car businesses that repaired electric systems.

Friendly man at the counter knew what I had in my hand before I could utter a word.

"Zener diode from a one-wire alternator. Seventeen bucks for a replacement. How many do you want?"

"One, I guess."

"Don't forget to clean every connection in your system or you'll be back here in a couple of days for another."

Armed with the new diode and precious advice, I returned to my sleek Jaguar and went to work. Before supper I had the refreshed alternator back on the engine and every connection in the system scrubbed clean. Most difficult was the ground strap that went to the frame rail. Corrosion around it from exposure to road debris caused me to raise an eyebrow. Was it the Achilles heel in the system? Causing consistent levels of resistance? Popping the diode on a regular basis? It was in such an awkward place that most mechanics wouldn't have gone to the effort of cleaning it by removing the stubborn anchor bolt and cleaning the corrosion.

Started the good looking Jag and watched the gauges come to life as the alternator could function as it should. Time for supper.

In the span of one day I had contacted a seller, examined his vehicle, assessed it, lowballed him, paid for it, took delivery, figured out what was wrong with it, fixed it; all before the evening meal. Day's work wasn't quite done.

After supper I phoned the classified departments of the large newspapers in Vancouver. This was Wednesday evening, the Province and Sun confirmed my ads would appear on Friday.

Two days later I received four phone calls. My well-worded adverts included the asking price of eighteen thousand, nine hundred and ninety-nine dollars.

Saturday morning had me in the underground parking lot with two gentlemen in their forties. They listened to the sleek Jaguar run but weren't really interested in going for a test drive. That told me one thing: not buyers.

An hour later and my next appointment, sharp dressed young man with a British accent. He too brought a friend. He loved the E-type and I let him and his pal drive around the block while I held the keys of his B.M.W. When they returned I had the right to ask him one question, "Would you like to buy my Jaguar?"

No beating around the bush, someone is interested enough to take a test drive, you need to ask if they will buy your car.

British man, "I love the Jag and I'd like to buy it. I'm here in Vancouver scouting investment opportunities for my mother and I need a vehicle. The 2+2 Jaguar is my favourite model of E-type. It will do nicely for my time in Vancouver but eighteen-nine is a little high. Can you move a bit on price?"

"My asking price is pretty fair, given the car's mileage and condition, but if you're sincere about buying it, I suppose I could let it go for eighteen and a half."

"How about seventeen even?"

"That's a little low."

We shook hands at seventeen and a half thousand (early 1990s) dollars. He didn't have that kind of money on his person. I wrote a bill of sale with all the particulars, including receipt of a thousand dollars in cash as a nonrefundable deposit to secure his purchase. Balance to be paid in full, upon delivery. That was the only fly in the ointment, as he had recently arrived in Vancouver he hadn't a bank account yet. It would take a few days to establish, and a few more to transfer funds (pre e-transfers of today) from England. A few days turned into two full weeks.

On a sunny Saturday morning I drove the beige Jag to a luxurious high-rise in an upscale neighbourhood of downtown Vancouver. Wife drove behind me in the fake-wood-panelled Pinto Pony station wagon.

In his apartment on the seventeenth floor, we finalized the official transfer form. He presented me with a certified cheque of sixteen thousand, five hundred dollars. I gave him the keys. Buyer and seller happy. Best type of deal.

A profit of just under ten thousand, six hundred dollars on a Jaguar that went from being a pain in one man's life to the pride and joy of another. I facilitated the deal by putting specific skills in action. A return of more than one-hundred percent was obtained.

Point is not to brag, merely to show that by having a clear idea and specific goals (before entering into any negotiation) you are already dealing from a position of strength. The ideal of doubling my money on every transaction was scoffed at by numerous peers, yet it was (and is) quite possible. Had I merely possessed some vague idea of wishing to make a profit on every deal, that's how I would have purchased and sold collector cars, and that is how it would have worked... vaguely.

Conversely, making thousands of dollars for very little effort happened on a regular basis. You can do the same by applying your expertise and specific (buying and selling) goals to whatever it is that excites you.

Sometimes a bit more effort was needed in order to realize the usual amount of profit on a deal. The next story is an example of such a transaction.

Lowballed Ferrari. After my job of managing an apartment building, I worked at a collector car restoration shop and found opportunities that very few would be interested in; projects that required a certain amount of effort to return a profit. Case in point — a 1965 Ferrari, 330 GTE, 2+2, four headlight coupé. Not the most coveted model of road car that Enzo Ferrari ever produced, but a V-12 powered 'Prancing Horse' nonetheless.

Heard about the vehicle from my employer. Bob brokered car deals as part of his job; putting buyer and seller together. He knew I was always looking for a project car that needed a specialist's touch. Bob was one of the people I told about my goal of making one hundred percent profit on every deal. On a regular basis Bob would snicker at the notion. Every few months, he might receive word of a possible project that required too much effort for him to bother to go and check out. A certain Ferrari fit the description.

Bob told me the facts: two brothers owned an old Ferrari. Both men (dentists) thought they were talented mechanics and decided to restore the Ferrari they had purchased some years before. Old car was in fair condition when they purchased it, bit of rust in the usual places, ran and drove like an average used car. The brothers were very enthused with their red Ferrari and eagerly wanted to restore it too perfect condition.

"How hard can it be... " one was heard to have said. They drove their Italian sports car into its new home; two car garage in back of one of the brothers' residences.

In a few weekends of feverish work. They stripped the car of everything they could lay wrenches on. Unlabelled parts were strewn high and low. I entered the garage and saw carburetors, upholstery, nuts, bolts; bits from the poor car spilled out of its trunk, on benches, on the floor... an explosion of the Italian mechanical parts everywhere. That wasn't the worst of it.

"Tell me the story of your Ferrari project," I asked the two dentists.

"We bought the car eight years ago..."

I could tell they hadn't been in the garage for many years. Cobwebs and dust were evident. They had the ability to strip a vehicle of its components but came to the realization fairly quick that they possessed neither the equipment, knowledge or patience to restore anything. In over their heads. Couldn't agree on a course of action. They paid too much money for the Ferrari initially to justify paying professionals to restore any of the parts that were languishing in their double garage. The only thing they could agree on; time to sell.

Adding insult to injury, someone broke into the garage five years previous and stole the Borrani, wire-wheels. What a mess; sitting on four jack-stands, the stripped Ferrari didn't look like much. Asking price? Forty-five thousand (early 1990s) dollars. A number you would pay for a decent model in good condition. This wasn't that car. I was interested but needed to carefully look at all the pieces to determine if anything else had gone missing when the rare wheels and tires did.

While examining the minefield of parts, I kept them talking with general questions to receive feedback that would indicate their level of motivation to sell. In between comments of, "Teenaged children learning to drive" and their spouses' teasing about the "Ferrari that can't move because it has no wheels." I carefully inspected the Ferrari and visualized the time, effort and money needed to bring it to the point of profitability.

Three of us spent an hour rummaging through the debris. Besides the missing 'knock-off, wire-wheels' and tires, I couldn't see any other pieces of the puzzle that needed to be sourced. All the while I busily calculated what amounts of time and money would be needed on my part to make the project worthwhile. Trying to keep my enthusiasm in check at the prospect of owning a Ferrari was part of the process. Had to stay focused on my goal: hundred percent profit. Could tell they were motivated.

Decided to make an offer.

"I might be able to do something with your project. I'm prepared to buy it today, in cash, value to me as it sits is fifteen-thousand."

I confidently put my offer on the table and shut my mouth. They looked at each other for a few seconds; one of them spoke.

"How 'bout twenty-five grand?"

In an instant they showed their level of determination in wanting to free themselves of their burden; a twenty thousand dollar drop in price. That told me they were ready to sell. I was there to solve their problem, just needed to establish a price that would make everyone happy.

Flatly stated, "I could do sixteen thousand."

I knew I could go as high as twenty thousand and still have a chance of doubling my investment of time and money.

"We might be able to let it go for twenty-two. Could you do that?"

The brothers were a tag-team, 'asking' me if I could stretch to their dollar figure. After a few more movements in price, we settled with handshakes. Eighteen and a half thousand dollars for a 1965, 330

GTE, 2+2, Ferrari project. I turned cartwheels in my mind. Outwardly I gave no emotion away. Poker face.

This happened on a Saturday morning. I paid them in cash from my Deal Bag (an actual, canvas banker's bag in the glove box of my Pinto station wagon that contained twenty five thousand dollars), filled out paperwork and hustled back to my workplace to borrow a set of four Borrani wheels from a Ferrari under restoration. The four-headlight Italian sports car would roll again, onto a flat deck tow truck.

Later that same day, my new project sat on jackstands in a quiet corner of the parking lot where I worked. Wrapped tightly in a weatherproof car cover. Waiting for my input of energy to bring it back to a semblance of its former glory. There it would sit, shedding rain, for a few months.

I had to earn the right to use the shop's facilities in my restoration of the Ferrari. To that end, I made a deal with Bob, my boss. He needed a mid-1950s, 180 SL Mercedes repainted. I volunteered my spare time/labour to his project. After work and weekends I dedicated time to Bob's Mercedes project. He was quite happy to see a shiny coat of black paint on his German car and the rust in its lower extremities properly repaired. My commitment of a few months complete.

I unwrapped the Ferrari and rolled it into the shop on its own set of Borrani, wire wheels. Was now able to use the shop's facilities.

One thousand (early 1990s) dollars is what it cost me to buy a set of wheels from a seller in Idaho, he had advertised in Hemming's Motor News, the Bible of any kind of car part your mind could imagine. A set of Michelin tires (with plenty of life and tread) just happened to fall into my possession, as the owner of a certain Mercedes was convinced he needed shiny new tires to go with a shiny new paint job. Funny how things work out.

Six months of work. That's what it took (evenings, after my regular shift and weekends) to have the Ferrari back on the road. Wouldn't even call it work, more of a joy, after an eight hour day of working for the man, I couldn't wait to lay hands on my project and use the shop's equipment after everyone had gone home.

Majority of the project was my labour. Kept an accurate tally of the hours and money spent. Couldn't go crazy creating an over-restored trailer-queen. Needed to have a decent looking car that drove well and could be sold for double my investment of time and money. Taking advantage of connections in my line of work was part of the exercise. As was knowing where and when to compromise in a sympathetic restoration.

People regularly spend many thousands of dollars to refresh a twelve cylinder Ferrari engine. That wasn't going to happen. Updating the valve-train with modern, neoprene valve stem seals (as sourced from a Mazda); that's a different story. Under fifty dollars for parts, and a vintage Ferrari cylinder head is fitted with seals that limit the amount of oil sucked into the cylinders during startup because the bronze valve guides are slightly worn. No more light puff of blue exhaust when firing those twelve cylinders to life. Insider 'gear-head' tricks that solve problems and save money. Becoming expert at what you do always pays dividends.

It turned out to be a wonderful car. Small amount of rust around the clutch and brake pedals was the trickiest bit to repair. Couldn't really understand why the dentists had stripped it for restoration instead of driving it for a few years first. I did something with the bright red, repainted Ferrari that most owners of such cars rarely do. Drove it; my daily driver for a full year.

Took great delight in putting the car through its paces. Like a thoroughbred, it was exercised, rain or shine, on my daily drive to work and numerous trips. Solid sports car; ran and drove as it should. Complete joy to let the high-revving V-12 engine and five-speed transmission run like they were meant to, instead of sitting in a garage collecting dust.

Word of my well-sorted Ferrari spread amongst fellow enthusiasts. I placed a couple of adverts in the local papers and let the voice spread that I was selling the 330 GTE. Asking price? Forty-five thousand dollars, a proper (early 1990s) amount for such a lovely driver.

Numerous phone calls. A few of the curious came and kicked the tires. I was looking for a serious buyer; someone with money, knowledge and enthusiasm. A fellow gear-head. Two weeks after my ads appeared, I had my man. We spoke the same language, even on the phone he was well-versed in the subtlety of Ferrari speak.

"To tell the truth Monty, I actually prefer Pininfarina's four-headlight look. He did the same for the Brits with the Austin Cambridge, back in the 1960s."

Rick was crazy about my car. Gave him the grand tour when he came to inspect my well-sorted ride. Showed him everything I did, under the chassis, under the hood, under the trunk carpet; every inch. Proper drive in a nice neighbourhood on curvy, smooth roads. Let him bond with it on the return drive as he felt the controls and how solid it was.

Returned to the sunny parking lot back at the shop. I asked him one question as we stood back and gazed at the handsome car, "Would you like to buy my Ferrari?"

"Yes."

Just had to settle on price. Bantering on the dollar figure was in my favour. I had established value by 'selling' the car. It was also priced at a realistic market value of forty-five thousand dollars.

Rick offered forty-two; we quickly shook hands at forty-three and a half thousand, to be paid in cash. He left me with a fifteen-hundred dollar, nonrefundable deposit. He would return in two days with the balance. Ferrari went to a good home after my stint as its custodian.

Conclusion. In the selling process, you must deal from a position of strength, just like buying. I knew my objective.

Accurate records of my time (including the hours on the Mercedes paint job) and total cash outlay for parts meant I had to sell the Ferrari for its market value of forty-five grand. At my sale price of forty-three and a half thousand, I realized a profit of over ninety percent. That paid me thirty-one dollars an hour for my labour. Double of what I made at my regular job. Plus; drove a Ferrari for a year. Not too bad for a blue-collar worker.

Lowball offers are about establishing the value of something you are attempting to purchase. Helping in that process is your level of expertise, confidence, being prepared to solve a person's problem immediately, having specific goals and sticking to your plan.

The selling process is very similar; you sell your customer on the value of whatever it is you have priced at a fair market rate. Very few people are so flush with money (and so foolish with it) that they will overpay for your item. You will usually be holding onto an overpriced car/painting/precious gem/piece of sports memorabilia or whatever for a long time if you try to make all your profit on the 'sale' side of a transaction. With each successful deal you will build confidence and learn more lessons about how to deal with people. Deal from a position of strength.

Addendum

Staying ahead of the big economic picture.

Every dog has its day. And so it is with shifts in global, economic supremacy, nothing stays the same. Change may be slow (wrought from within) or cataclysmic and brought about by natural or man-made forces. Either way, being aware of changes in the world's economically strong and weak nations will keep you informed of major trends. Information is power; being empowered will help you deal from a position of strength. That's what this addendum is about; informing yourself about the big picture so your decisions at a local level are profitable.

History is littered with the ruins of great societies, nations that enjoyed many seasons as the big dog on the block. Incan, Mayan, Persian, Egyptian, Greek, Roman, Spanish, Dutch, French and British civilizations are a few examples of peoples that enjoyed being the most powerful and wealthy amongst their peers. Here's the thing, it's tough at the top. As many nations have learned, it is very expensive to keep a large military fed and equipped, ready to defend one's borders. More costly are wars of extractive or imperial design. When the number one nation has to assume huge amounts of debt just to maintain its armed forces... you know it is on a downward slide.

In modern times the ability to observe the 'rich country syndrome' is fairly easy. A wealthy western nation spawns multiple generations of entitled offspring. Fifty to a hundred years of being number one produces an atmosphere of laziness. Workers demand more for their labour, forcing business owners to make tough decisions. Meanwhile, hungrier countries have been envious of the wealthy nation's lifestyle and want a piece of the pie. Without anyone pinpointing an exact moment in time, a transition has started; a global shift in wealth and power.

Manufacturing jobs (the backbone of a country's wealth) flow to different areas of the globe where labour costs and regulations are far less. Former workers in 'fat cat nation' still demand to live in the style they feel they have been entitled to, and their government agrees. Subsidies, food stamps, welfare, unemployment benefits and numerous programs funded by the state only add to the nation's debt. Couple that with the budget of maintaining the world's largest military and the amount of debt becomes unsustainable.

It should be obvious that we are talking about the United States of America. At this point in time (2015) a major transition has been underway for many years; the West is losing jobs, wealth and power to the East.

Unless radical changes are made at every level of governance and from the ground up, the trend will continue. You, as a participant in your local economy can benefit from knowledge of the shift in global activity as it impacts your day-to-day transactions. Applying that information in a positive way starts with information of how things have evolved.

For a number of decades North American factories have relocated to China and other oriental countries. These brick-and-mortar businesses have been replaced at an alarming rate by a 'smoke and mirrors' economy of financial services. Through numerous legislative flip-flops (repeal of the Glass-Steagall Act in 1999, etc.) Wall Street, Bay Street and highflying financial institutes have been given ample latitude to invent thinly veiled con games that are passed off as investments. Money shuffles that profit the inventors of the game more than the investors.

Fancy titles that tend to confuse rather than clarify: Credit Default Swaps, Derivatives, Subprime loans, Mortgage backed Securities, de-securitized hedge funds, Registered Education Investment Trusts; there are thousands of such vehicles. Investing in sophisticated paper games has become something of an industry. The fact that Wall Street investment banks have access to the man on the street and his savings, means more people are swept up in polished proposals, then spat out as losers when events halfway around the globe create a downward domino-effect of loss that comes back to take a huge bite out of their investment. Not a position of strength.

Same holds true for stock-markets; odds are stacked heavily against you. The house tends to win more often than the small player. As most markets in North America are subject to machinations of large interests (read; manipulation) brought about by an alliance of the Federal Reserve, Wall Street, too-big-to-fail banks, government insiders and mainstream media. You owe it to yourself to be aware of how the bigger game of finance is tilted heavily in favour of the tiny percentage of the population that actually set all the rules.

With the continual erosion of real industry and manufacturing in North America (while more services of a financial nature pop-up) there is greater effort put forth to find slick ways to help you part with your money. Buying any paper investment, in my opinion, is to operate from a position of weakness. Relinquishing control of hard earned money to some outside source is foolish.

A position of strength when investing is always accomplished when you control the outcome. Should some event halfway around the world cause a ripple of fallout that cuts North American stock-markets by forty percent overnight, you can deal from a position of strength by standing back and picking up real assets for pennies on the dollar; or you can watch helplessly while your portfolio takes a massive hit. My advice; invest in yourself, not stocks or any of the many paper products being foisted onto people with a bit of savings.

Part of the process of investing in yourself is keeping informed of world affairs. How can events in China, Russia, Europe or anywhere else for that matter, affect you and your family? Will the threat of war or sanctions by America on trade with Russia affect the price of gasoline you put in your car? Do you live where you work and don't commute? Will a price war amongst oil-producing countries (OPEC) lower fuel prices so you can fill the five-hundred gallon tank on your hobby farm and be able to operate equipment for a six months while prices rise? Can you wait in the wings (knowing that easy credit and a glut of new houses on the market has created an unsustainable bubble in real estate) and then purchase a house when its price has dropped thirty percent?

International and domestic big-picture (macroeconomic) factors can unfold overnight and affect many aspects of your local market. The vast majority of people are poorly informed about anything developing in world affairs, they're more concerned about their 'earn and consume' existence and are quite shocked when a sequence of events causes their home to be devalued by a third. Couple that with a rapid rise in interest rates and many mortgage payers struggle to make payments on a house they are suddenly 'upside down' in; committed to paying for an edifice that is worth less than their purchase price.

Avoiding such situations, that victimize and force you to deal from a position of weakness, only requires a bit of study. Proper information is the key. Truthful details on economic trends rarely come from any level of government or the mainstream media. Politicians are (for the most part) usually concerned with being re-elected, going to great lengths to paint a rosy economic picture by massaging data that casts them (and their party) in a better light. Same holds true for the majority of media in North America (television, radio and newspapers); most sources are owned by a small group of people and information emanating through the mainstream will have a bias that reflects the proprietors' ideology. Both areas of general information should be viewed with a healthy level of skepticism. They have been known to report "all is well" with the economy, right up to the moment of a cataclysmic crash, then claim no one could have seen it coming.

You are better served seeking unbiased information from freelance sources that aren't bought-and-paid-for journalistic shills, the so-called Presstitutes. There is no need to sit in front of a computer for hours each day (in order to distill a mountain of misinformation and propaganda) there are people that do it for you. They gladly post blogs from sources around the world that are eyewitnesses to real events. Your job is to balance their reportage with other sources in order to receive the most accurate assessment of reality.

I have my favourite websites (and learned people) I access for a few minutes each day. They keep me ahead of the curve. Advance notice of a continual buildup of 'Federal Reserve easy credit' and the resultant bubbles in stocks, bonds, equities and real estate is just one of many areas that prepare the savvy student to operate from a position of strength.

It is also beneficial to be informed of your government's true level of indebtedness, both locally and as a nation. Excess debt and borrowing will be paid for in many ways; governments seem to always need more funds to pay for services being demanded by their electorate, those costs are usually passed down to the working men and women: higher taxes, user fees, elevated prices for permits and everyday items that are subject to taxation, i.e. gasoline, road tolls, parking, cuts in pension benefits; basically, anything under jurisdiction of government will usually rise in price.

Being aware of monies that were once earmarked for infrastructure and education that are being used to service interest on municipal bonds will give you insights that most people don't concern themselves with. It can mean the difference between purchasing a property in a fiscally healthier municipality on the other side of town or, the other side of the country.

Taking a small amount of time on a regular basis to study the writings and reports of unbiased people on a variety of websites will provide you with ample insight of world events that affect the economy. It is not within the scope of this book to give actual names of people I have come to respect for their knowledge, as they may or may not be around when you read this. Your task is to research numerous sources until you have found trustworthy information, then... never stop asking questions. When extraordinary claims are made; extraordinary evidence must be presented. There are all sorts of pundits and talking heads that make numerous predictions on which way the economy will go, their forecasts are usually of 'boom or bust' scenarios of exaggerated hype, backed by very little evidence. Avoiding the noise of loud voices (that contain little substance) becomes quite easy when you have taken the time to study serious writings of authors that insist you ask questions and make up your own mind based on evidence put forward.

Armed with valid information of world market trends and their affect on your local economy (and coupled with Deal Bag money) you are in a powerful position to bargain. Align that with your expertise, confidence and specific goals will ensure that you have a decided advantage of building lasting wealth compared to the majority of indebted people who survive from paycheque to paycheque.

Most people don't have a financial plan, don't have specific objectives, have never set or accomplished any goals, have no idea what is happening in local or international markets, would never consider any amount of sacrifice or frugal living (to earn a long-term return on their effort) and don't think twice about more personal debt. The fact you have read this far indicates you're serious about transforming your minimum wage into maximum wealth. It can be done.

True motivation to accomplish anything worthwhile comes from within; I can't thrust it upon you, nobody can. Wanting something and then acting upon that desire (in a positive way) is what separates truly motivated people from those that merely wish for something. With the tools, rules and instructions outlined in Blue-Collar Riches you will have an excellent start on the road to building real wealth.

You can now deal from a position of strength.

Chapter Seven

Conclusion

Turned out my ex-wife did me a favour many years ago when she went ballistic in the bank by not signing mortgage papers on my first real estate deal. I didn't know it at the time; my mind was clouded by anger, frustration and murderous fantasies. In retrospect she inadvertently pushed me from creating wealth in real estate to a pursuit of my true passion: cool cars. Buying, fixing and reselling vintage vehicles in my spare time evolved into a specialized, full-time career of aluminum coach-building. My one-man shop where I handcrafted aluminum body panels for customers' valuable collector cars.

Developing the skills to accurately replicate repair panels by hand and install them on handmade, vintage automobiles started with an intense course of self-instruction. A two-year, full-time project that cost me every dime that I had accumulated in my Deal Bag: fifty-five thousand (1994) dollars. I embarked on a very ambitious project to create my own Maserati-powered, aluminum-bodied, handmade sports car. (Google 'Monty McGale' and proceed to 'Maserati enthusiasts page' for further details).

Sacrifice of living like a pauper, where every dollar was stretched to the max while I lived in the tiny attic space of my rented garage was part of the plan. Everyone thought I had gone bonkers. Twenty-four months of teaching myself the art and skill of hand-forming aluminum panels. Using an English wheel and gas-welding (oxyacetylene) aluminum is an old skill that very few people possess in this era of instant everything.

After two years of effort, working full-time and living off my savings, I had built a beautiful sports car of my own design. The Maserati Powered Special garnered much attention, winning numerous accolades at car shows.

Floodgates opened. My little two-car garage was busy for many years with a steady stream of customers who paid me a premium wage to repair/restore/rebuild the bodywork of their valued collector cars. I specialized in repairing the rare, aluminum-bodied sports cars of Italian and British marques.

As I worked hard, lived frugally and invested the majority of each month's income, the genesis of Blue-Collar Riches formed in my mind. Helping to guide my thought-process was continual questioning of my wealthy clients. Insights about investing and protecting wealth helped point me in the right direction with regard to placing money where it can do the most and allow the investor to sleep soundly at night.

After using my Maserati Special as a daily driver for five years, it was sold to a good home in Belgium. Money from the sale went into my favourite area of investment; precious metals. Gold and silver bullion and coins. Early 2001 proved to be an opportune time to start converting dollars into precious metals. For numerous years I faithfully exchanged the majority of my cash income for gold and silver. Value of precious metals (expressed in dollars) has multiplied manyfold over the years since then; ensuring savings will be available for future use.

At the age of fifty I decided (more or less) to retire. Beating shape into metal panels by hand is a very physical occupation; writing books... not so much. (Although I know from experience which vocation pays better!)

My present girlfriend and I enjoy a comfortable lifestyle. I possess a modest duplex that was paid for without a mortgage, collect rent from tenants that are willing to pay a premium for upscale accommodations and am free to pursue anything that interests me.

We don't live like millionaires, spending money like it grows on trees. Our continual goal is to squeeze the best value from every dollar; old habits die hard. Because we took the initiative in earlier years to prepare for the future, a certain level of comfort has been attained. By adhering to the principles of Blue-

Collar Riches as a starting point, you can do the same.

Thanks for reading.

www.ingramcontent.com/pod-product-compliance
Lightning Source LLC
Chambersburg PA
CBHW021423170526
45164CB00001B/67